Countdown to Christmas

Quilts and More
That Span the Seasons

Susan Ache

Martingale
Create with Confidence

Countdown to Christmas:
Quilts and More That Span the Seasons
© 2019 by Susan Ache

Martingale®
19021 120th Ave. NE, Ste. 102
Bothell, WA 98011-9511 USA
ShopMartingale.com

Printed in China
24 23 22 21 20 19   8 7 6 5 4 3 2 1

Library of Congress Cataloging-in-Publication Data is available upon request.

ISBN: 978-1-60468-994-5

MISSION STATEMENT

We empower makers who use fabric and yarn to make life more enjoyable.

CREDITS

PUBLISHER AND CHIEF VISIONARY OFFICER
Jennifer Erbe Keltner

CONTENT DIRECTOR
Karen Costello Soltys

MANAGING EDITOR
Tina Cook

TECHNICAL EDITOR
Elizabeth Beese

COPY EDITOR
Marcy Heffernan

DESIGN MANAGER
Adrienne Smitke

PRODUCTION MANAGER
Regina Girard

COVER AND BOOK DESIGNER
Kathy Kotomaimoce

PHOTOGRAPHER
Brent Kane

ILLUSTRATOR
Missy Shepler

SPECIAL THANKS
Photography for this book was taken at the home of Julie Thomas in Maltby, Washington (Instagram: @littlefarmstead).

Susan Rogers machine quilted the projects in this book.

Contents

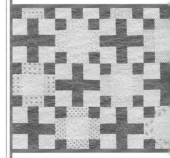

Introduction   5

PROJECTS

Christmas Vacation   7

Irma 450   13

O Christmas Tree   19

Granny's Gift   25

Tussy Mussy Christmas   33

Ho Ho Ho   41

Christmas Welcome   47

Tree Farming   53

Peppermint Party   59

Tiddlywinks   65

Background Music   71

Crisscross Applesauce   75

About the Author   *80*

There's more online! Find free bonus patterns for a Tussy Mussy Pillow and a Background Music Pillow at ShopMartingale.com/CountdowntoChristmas.

Introduction

Decorating and making quilts for the holidays is something I love. But making a lap or bed quilt just for Christmas may seem like a big undertaking, only to box up the quilt and put it away for 11 months of the year.

Which is exactly why I don't do that! As you page through this book, my hope is that you'll find pictures of quilts that you'd love to have in your home. And I hope you notice that, aside from a few exceptions, while these quilts make wonderful backdrops for the season, they aren't overtly what I'd call "Christmas quilts." They may feature red or green or both, but the colors are soft and they blend well with many of the other quilts I use in my home, which makes it easy for me to display them on shelves, layered on beds, or draped over cozy sofas and chairs year-round.

I love to mix and mingle—and not just at holiday parties. While you may not display the Ho Ho Ho quilt (page 41) all year long, many of the others are perfect for mingling on guest beds, in your favorite reading nook, or on top of a big stack of favorite quilts. Even in July!

So I encourage you do to what I like to do. In the beginning of a new year, when all the decorations and gifts are put away and the house is cleaned up and back to normal, I start sewing quilts like these. As soon as I've completed one, I can start using it. Then I may make another. And when the next Christmas season rolls around, you can bet those quilts are going to move to center stage!

Cheers,

Susan

Christmas Vacation

QUILT SIZE: 62½" × 75½" BLOCK SIZE: 11" × 11"

 Every Thanksgiving Day, my family brings out the one movie that starts our entire Christmas season, *National Lampoon's Christmas Vacation.* Everybody can quote all of the lines before they actually happen, and we still laugh like it's our first time watching it. This movie will be played about every other day in our house, so it would be doing my family a disservice if I didn't include a quilt to honor the movie that starts our Christmas countdown. Instead of piecing the border separately and adding it after making the quilt center, I sewed it at the same time I pieced the center, so it was "one and done."

Materials

Yardage is based on 42"-wide fabric. Fat eighths are 9" × 21".

40 fat eighths of assorted red prints for blocks, sashing, inner border, and outer border

45 fat eighths of assorted light prints for blocks, sashing, inner border, and outer border

⅝ yard of red tone on tone for binding

4⅝ yards of fabric for backing

69" × 82" piece of batting

Cutting

All measurements include ¼" seam allowances.

From the assorted red prints, cut:

18 strips, 3½" × 21"; crosscut into:
　18 strips, 3½" × 11½"
　20 squares, 3½" × 3½"
　12 rectangles, 1½" × 3½"
80 strips, 1½" × 21"; crosscut *40 of the strips* into:
　124 rectangles, 1½" × 2½"
　280 squares, 1½" × 1½"

From the assorted light prints, cut:

34 strips, 2½" × 21"; crosscut into:
　49 strips, 2½" × 9½"
　22 rectangles, 2½" × 3½"
　34 squares, 2½" × 2½"
126 strips, 1½" × 21"; crosscut *86 of the strips* into:
　18 strips, 1½" × 11½"
　80 strips, 1½" × 7½"
　80 strips, 1½" × 5½"
　80 rectangles, 1½" × 3½"
　44 squares, 1½" × 1½"

From the red tone on tone, cut:

8 strips, 2½" × 42"

Susan says...

Despite having the words "Christmas Vacation" in its name, this quilt stays on display year-round at my house. It may not be in the most prominent position every month of the year, but it doesn't live in a closet! Because I didn't use holiday prints, the soft reds and creams blend nicely with many of my other quilts. I encourage you to do a quilt shuffle too. Rearrange your stacks and displays, and they'll look fresh and new!

Making the Blocks

Press the seam allowances as indicated by the arrows.

1 Sew together one red and one light print 1½" × 21" strip to make strip set A. Make 40 of strip set A. From each strip set, crosscut 11 A segments, 1½" wide (440 total).

Make 40 A strip sets, 2½" x 21".
Cut 440 A segments, 1½" x 2½".

2 Sew together an A segment and a red 1½" square to make a B segment. Make 40 B segments.

Make 40 B segments,
1½" x 3½".

3 Sew together two A segments and a light 1½" square to make a C segment. Make 40 C segments.

Make 40 C segments,
1½" x 5½".

8 Sew together two A segments and a light 1½" × 7½" strip to make a H segment. Make 40 H segments.

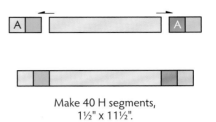

Make 40 H segments,
1½" x 11½".

9 Sew B segments to opposite sides of a red print 3½" square. Sew C segments to the top and bottom. Press. Working alphabetically, continue to add D, E, and F segments as shown. Sew light 1½" × 7½" strips to the sides. Then add G and H segments to the top and bottom to complete a block; press. Repeat to make 20 blocks that measure 11½" square, including seam allowances.

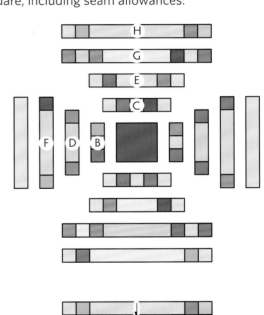

Make 20 blocks,
11½" x 11½".

4 Sew together two red 1½" squares and a light 1½" × 3½" strip to make a D segment. Make 40 D segments.

Make 40 D segments,
1½" x 5½".

5 Sew together two A segments and a light 1½" × 3½" strip to make an E segment. Make 40 E segments.

Make 40 E segments,
1½" x 7½".

6 Sew together two red 1½" squares and a light 1½" × 5½" strip to make an F segment. Make 40 F segments.

Make 40 F segments,
1½" x 7½".

7 Sew together two red 1½" squares, two A segments, and one light 1½" × 5½" strip to make a G segment. Make 40 G segments.

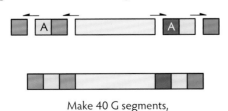

Make 40 G segments,
1½" x 11½".

2 Join two red 1½" × 2½" rectangles and a light 2½" × 9½" rectangle as shown to make a sashing rectangle. Make 49 sashing rectangles.

Make 49 sashing rectangles,
2½" x 11½".

3 To make the top border row, lay out two border corners, two red 1½" × 3½" rectangles, five light 2½" × 3½" rectangles, and four red 3½" × 11½" strips in a row as shown. Join the pieces to make a border row. The row should measure 3½" × 62½", including seam allowances. Repeat to make the bottom border row.

Make 2 border rows,
3½" x 62½".

4 To make a narrow sashing row, lay out two red 1½" × 3½" rectangles, two light 1½" squares, five red 1½" × 2½" rectangles, and four light 1½" × 11½" strips in a row as shown. Join the pieces to make a narrow sashing row. The row should measure 1½" × 62½", including seam allowances. Repeat to make a second narrow sashing row.

Make 2 narrow sashing rows,
1½" x 62½".

5 To make a wide sashing row, lay out two light 2½" × 3½" rectangles, two red 1½" × 2½" rectangles, five light 2½" squares, and four sashing rectangles in a row as shown. Join the pieces to make a wide sashing row. The row should measure 2½" × 62½", including seam allowances. Repeat to make six wide sashing rows.

Make 6 wide sashing rows,
2½" x 62½".

Assembling the Quilt Top

Instead of piecing the blocks and borders separately, I put the entire quilt together in 15 horizontal rows. This leaves less room for error than piecing the side borders first and then attaching them to the quilt center.

1 Sew a red 1½" × 2½" rectangle to one side of a light 2½" square. Add a red 1½" × 3½" rectangle to the adjacent side as shown to make a border corner. Make four border corners, each 3½" square, including seam allowances.

Make 4 border corners,
3½" x 3½".

6 To make a block row, lay out two red 3½" × 11½" strips, two light 1½" × 11½" strips, five sashing rectangles, and four blocks in a row as shown. Join the pieces to make a block row. The row should measure 11½" × 62½", including seam allowances. Repeat to make five block rows.

Make 5 block rows,
11½" x 62½".

7 Referring to the quilt assembly diagram below, sew together the border rows, narrow and wide sashing rows, and block rows to make the quilt top, which should measure 62½" × 75½", including seam allowances.

Finishing the Quilt

Find free, detailed finishing instructions online at ShopMartingale.com/HowtoQuilt.

1 Prepare the quilt backing so it's about 6" larger in both directions than the quilt top.

2 Layer the backing, batting, and quilt top. Baste the layers together.

3 Hand or machine quilt as desired; the quilt shown is machine quilted with an allover flower-and-leaf design.

4 Using the red tone-on-tone 2½"-wide strips, make the binding and attach it to the quilt.

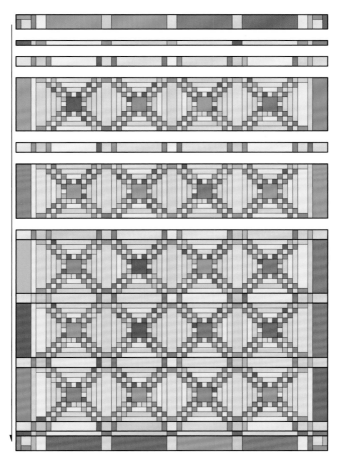

Quilt assembly

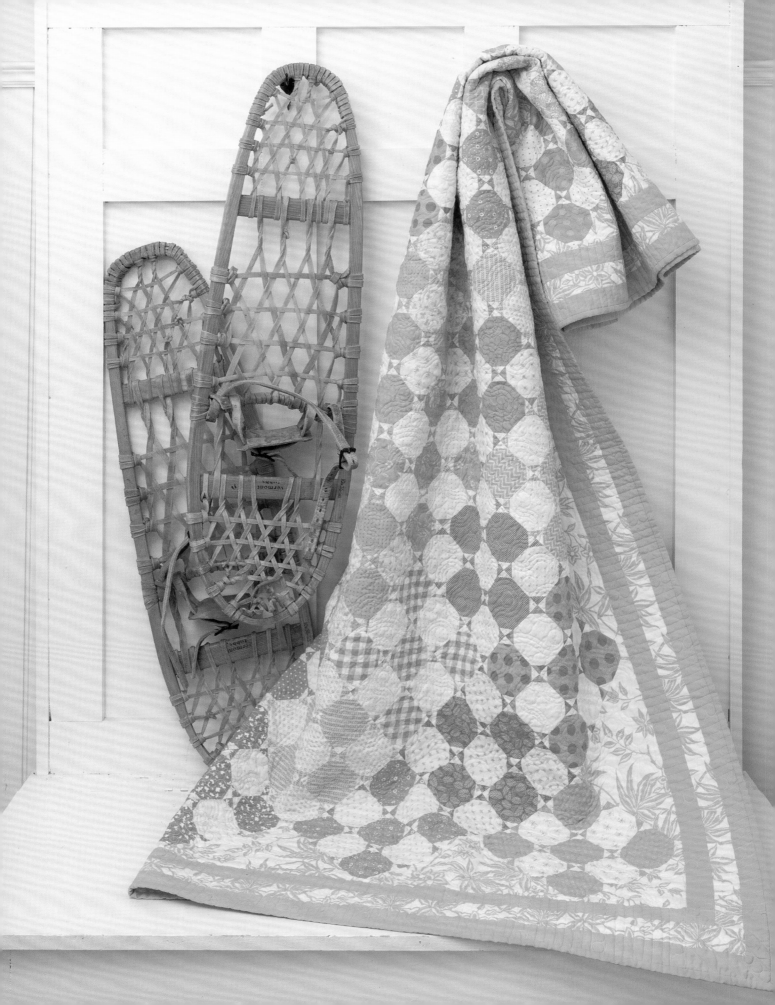

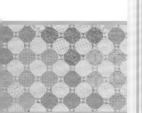
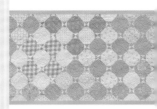

Irma 450

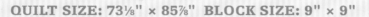

QUILT SIZE: 73⅛" × 85⅞" BLOCK SIZE: 9" × 9"

 You can probably think of a dozen cute Christmas names for this wonderfully snowball-laden quilt, but the summer of 2017 was a rough hurricane season in Florida. During this time, the Weather Channel stayed on 24/7, we bought hurricane provisions and great junk food, and we made preparations in the yard and house. And while the electricity was still on, I sewed and sewed and sewed—450 snowballs to be exact! So while another quilt name might be more appropriate for Christmas, this quilt will forever be known as "Irma 450," named for the storm that barreled through my state.

Materials

Yardage is based on 42"-wide fabric. Fat quarters are 18" × 21".

20 fat quarters of assorted light prints for blocks
20 fat quarters of assorted green prints for blocks
1⅞ yards of cream print for side and corner setting
   triangles and border
1⅝ yards of light green solid for borders and binding
6⅞ yards of fabric for backing
82" × 94" piece of batting

Cutting

All measurements include ¼" seam allowances. Before cutting, pair each light print fat quarter with a green print fat quarter. (You should have 20 pairs.) From 10 of these pairs, you will be making 2 A blocks and 1 B block. From the remaining 10 pairs, you will be making 1 A block and 1 B block. Cut fabrics as specified below, then keep all pieces from each pair together.

From the light print in *each of the first 10 pairs*, cut:
3 strips, 3½" × 21"; crosscut into 13 squares,
   3½" × 3½" (130 total)
4 strips, 1¼" × 21"; crosscut into 56 squares,
   1¼" × 1¼" (560 total)

From the green print in *each of the first 10 pairs*, cut:
3 strips, 3½" × 21"; crosscut into 14 squares,
   3½" × 3½" (140 total)
4 strips, 1¼" × 21"; crosscut into 52 squares,
   1¼" × 1¼" (520 total)

From the light print in *each of the last 10 pairs*, cut:
2 strips, 3½" × 21"; crosscut into 9 squares,
   3½" × 3½" (90 total)
3 strips, 1¼" × 21"; crosscut into 36 squares,
   1¼" × 1¼" (360 total)

From the green print in *each of the last 10 pairs*, cut:
2 strips, 3½" × 21"; crosscut into 9 squares,
   3½" × 3½" (90 total)
3 strips, 1¼" × 21"; crosscut into 36 squares,
   1¼" × 1¼" (360 total)

Continued on page 14

Continued from page 13

From the cream print, cut:

5 squares, 15" × 15"; cut the squares into quarters diagonally to yield 20 setting triangles (2 will be extra)

2 squares, 8" × 8"; cut the squares in half diagonally to yield 4 corner triangles

8 strips, 2" × 42"

From the light green solid, cut:

9 strips, 2½" × 42"

15 strips, 2" × 42"

Making the Blocks

Press the seam allowances as indicated by the arrows. Referring to the following instructions, make two A blocks and one B block from each of the first 10 pairs of fabrics you sorted in the fabric cutting section. Then make one A block and one B block from each of the second group of pairs.

1 Use a pencil to mark a diagonal line on the wrong side of each light and green 1¼" square.

2 Align a marked light square right sides together in one corner of a green 3½" square as shown. Sew on the drawn line. Trim the seam allowances to ¼" and press the resulting triangle toward the green square. Add three more matching marked squares in the same manner to make a dark unit, which should measure 3½" square, including seam allowances. Repeat to make five matching dark units.

Make 5 matching dark units,
3½" x 3½".

3 Using the same prints as in step 2, use four marked green 1¼" squares and one light 3½" square to make a light unit; note that the seam allowances are pressed toward the green corner triangles, which is the opposite direction as the dark units. Make four matching light units.

Make 4 matching light units,
3½" x 3½".

4 Lay out five dark units and four light units all with the same prints in three rows as shown. Sew together the units in each row, and then join the rows to make block A. Repeat to make 30 A blocks, each 9½" square, including seam allowances.

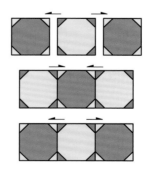
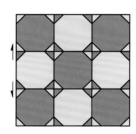

Make 30 A blocks,
9½" x 9½".

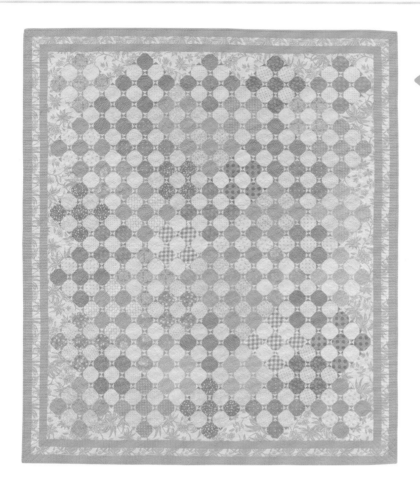

Susan says...

Snowball blocks are easy to make—and they pile up quickly, just like snow during a blizzard! (Or so I've heard.) I like to mark as many of the small squares as I can in one sitting so that I'm ready to chain piece blocks whenever I'm near my sewing machine. I'm already itching to make another version of this quilt in shades of blue and white.

5 In the same manner as for block A, use one light print and one green print to make five light units and four dark units.

Make 5 matching light units, 3½" x 3½".

Make 4 matching dark units, 3½" x 3½".

6 Lay out five light units and four dark units all with the same prints in three rows as shown. Sew together the units in each row, and then join the rows to make block B. Repeat to make 20 B blocks, each 9½" square, including seam allowances.

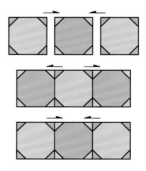

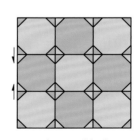

Make 20 B blocks, 9½" x 9½".

Assembling the Quilt Top

1 Referring to the quilt assembly diagram, lay out the blocks, side setting triangles, and corner setting triangles in diagonal rows. Note that the side and corner triangles are oversized and will be trimmed after assembly. Sew together the blocks and triangles in each row.

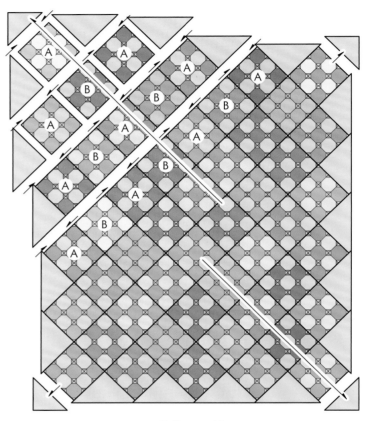

Quilt assembly

2 Join the rows and add the corner triangles. Carefully trim the excess from the setting triangles, ¼" beyond the points of the blocks. The quilt top should measure 64⅛" × 76⅞", including seam allowances.

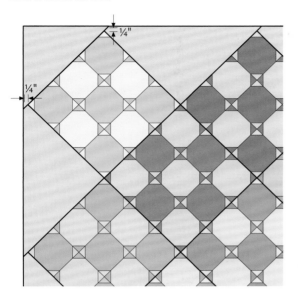

Adding the Borders

1 Join the light green solid 2" × 42" strips end to end and press the seam allowances open. Trim the pieced length into two 82⅞"-long outer-border strips, two 73⅛"-long outer-border strips, two 76⅞"-long inner-border strips, and two 67⅛"-long inner-border strips.

2 Join the cream 2" × 42" strips end to end and press the seam allowances open. Trim the pieced length into two 79⅞"-long middle-border strips and two 70⅛"-long middle-border strips.

3 Sew the longer inner-border strips to the sides of the quilt top, and then add the shorter strips to the top and bottom edges. Repeat to add the middle- and outer-border strips. The completed quilt top should measure 73⅛" × 85⅞".

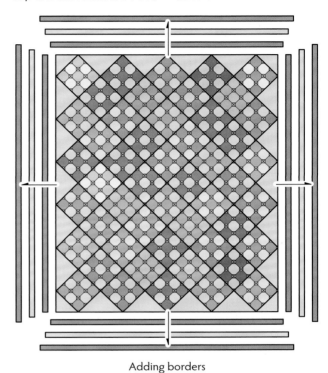

Adding borders

Finishing the Quilt

Find free, detailed finishing instructions online at ShopMartingale.com/HowtoQuilt.

1 Prepare the quilt backing so it is about 8" larger in both directions than the quilt top.

2 Layer the backing, batting, and quilt top. Baste the layers together.

3 Hand or machine quilt as desired; the quilt shown is machine quilted with an allover circle-and-spiral design in the blocks and with straight lines and circles in the border.

4 Using the light green solid 2½"-wide strips, make the binding and attach it to the quilt.

O Christmas Tree

QUILT SIZE: 55½" × 55½" BLOCK SIZE: 5" × 5"

 Many of us have special family memories involving a Christmas tree. Mine are of decorating the tree when my children were young. Most of the tree was decorated at my waist height. My husband is the lights and garland guy. The only help he requires is for us to stand back and ooh and ahh.

This is a great green scrap-buster quilt. Please don't even think about matching—if it's green, let it play in your Christmas tree. I love red ornaments, but this is a terrific opportunity to grab 5" charm squares and decorate in any colors you like.

Materials

Yardage is based on 42"-wide fabric. Fat quarters are 18" × 21". Fat eighths are 9" × 21".

16 fat quarters of assorted green prints for blocks

10 fat quarters of assorted white prints for blocks and quilt background

20 squares, 5" × 5", of assorted red prints for ornament appliqués

2 fat eighths of different gold prints for star

2 fat eighths of different brown prints for tree trunk

1¾ yards of red floral for border and binding

3½ yards of fabric for backing

62" × 62" square of batting

Template plastic

Freezer paper

Cutting

All measurements include ¼" seam allowances. Trace the triangle pattern on page 24 onto template plastic and cut out the shape on the drawn lines. Trace the template onto the wrong side of the fabrics specified below, rotating the template 180° after each cut to make the best use of your fabric.

From the assorted green prints, cut:

16 strips, 3" × 21"; crosscut into 80 triangles (refer to diagram below)

115 strips, 1" × 21"

Cut 5 triangles per strip.

From the assorted white prints, cut:

23 strips, 3" × 21"; crosscut into:
28 triangles
102 squares, 3" × 3"

1 square, 3⅜" × 3⅜"; cut the square in half diagonally to yield 2 small triangles

From *each* gold print, cut:

4 squares, 3⅜" × 3⅜"; cut the squares in half diagonally to yield 8 small triangles (16 total)

From *each* brown print, cut:

1 strip, 3" × 21"; crosscut into 2 triangles (4 total)

From scraps of one brown print, cut:

2 strips, 1½" × 5½"

Continued on page 20

3 Choose four pieced triangles—two with the seam allowances pressed toward the narrow point and two with the seam allowances pressed toward the wide base. Lay out these triangles in pairs so each abuts a triangle with the seam allowances running in the opposite direction. Sew the triangles in pairs as shown. Join the pairs to make a pieced green Hourglass block. Refer to the tip below to press the seam allowances in the directions shown. Make 20 green Hourglass blocks, each 5½" square, including seam allowances.

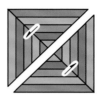

Make 20 blocks,
5½" x 5½".

Continued from page 19

From the red floral, cut:
1 square, 5⅞" × 5⅞"; cut the square in half diagonally to yield 2 large triangles
2 strips, 5½" × 40½"
2 strips, 5½" × 24½"
2 strips, 5½" × 23"
6 strips, 2½" × 42"
2 squares, 3⅜" × 3⅜"; cut the squares in half diagonally to yield 4 small triangles
2 squares, 3" × 3"

Making the Strip-Pieced Green Hourglass Blocks

Press the seam allowances as indicated by the arrows.

1 Sew together five assorted green print 1" × 21" strips to make a strip set. Make 23 strip sets.

Make 23 strip sets, 3" x 21".

2 Referring to the diagram, use the triangle template to cut 113 strip-pieced triangles.

Cut 113 pieced green triangles.

Pressing Trick

To press all the seam allowances of the Hourglass blocks in one direction (clockwise when looking at the back of the block), remove the stitches above the horizontal seam joining the two halves.

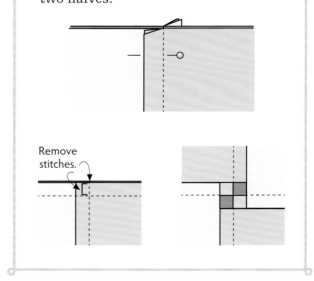

Remove stitches.

Making the Ornament Blocks

1 Join four assorted green triangles to make a green Hourglass block. Repeat to make 20 green Hourglass blocks that are 5½" square, including seam allowances.

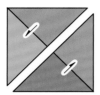

Make 20 blocks,
5½" x 5½".

2 Using the circle pattern on page 24, trace the shape 20 times onto the dull side of freezer paper. Cut out the freezer-paper circles on the drawn lines.

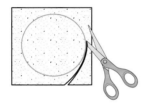

3 Using a hot, dry iron, press each freezer-paper circle onto the wrong side of a red print 5" square. Cut out each fabric circle, adding a ¼" seam allowance beyond the freezer paper.

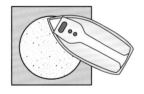

4 Using the tip of your iron, press the seam allowance over the edge of each freezer-paper circle to the wrong side.

5 Center a prepared circle on a green Hourglass block. Using a narrow zigzag stitch, sew the circle in place. Remove the freezer paper when you have about one-third of the distance left to stitch, or carefully cut out the backing, leaving a ¼" seam allowance, and then pull out the paper. Make 20 Ornament blocks.

Make 20 blocks,
5½" x 5½".

Making the Remaining Units

1 Choose two strip-pieced triangles—one with the seam allowances pressed toward the narrow point and one with the seam allowances pressed toward the wide base. Join these triangles and two white print triangles in pairs as shown, sewing their short edges together. Join the pairs to make a white-and-green Hourglass block. Repeat the pressing trick from page 20 in order to press all seam allowances as shown. Make 14 blocks, each 5½" square, including seam allowances.

Make 14 blocks,
5½" x 5½".

2 Using a large red floral triangle instead of the two white triangles, repeat step 1 to make a red-and-green Hourglass block. Make two.

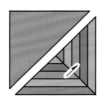

Make 2 blocks,
5½" x 5½".

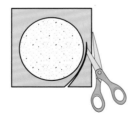

3 Using brown triangles, repeat step 1 to make a brown Hourglass block.

Make 1 block,
5½" x 5½".

4 Sew small triangles from each of the gold prints together to make a gold half-square-triangle unit. Make four, each 3" square, including seam allowances.

Make 4 units,
3" x 3".

5 Using the triangle colors specified, repeat step 4 to make two gold-and-red half-square-triangle units from each gold print and one white-and-gold unit from each gold print.

Make 2.   Make 1.   Make 2.   Make 1.

6 Sew small gold triangles to the short edges of the remaining pieced green triangle as shown. The unit should measure 3" × 5½", including seam allowances.

Make 1 unit,
3" x 5½".

Assembling the Quilt Top

Referring to the quilt assembly diagram, lay out the blocks, assorted white 3" squares, and the remaining units in 10 horizontal rows. First join the squares in the sections beside the Hourglass blocks and press as shown. Sew each pair of these rows together. Then join the white partial rows and the blocks in each horizontal row. Sew the rows. The quilt top should measure 45½" square, including seam allowances.

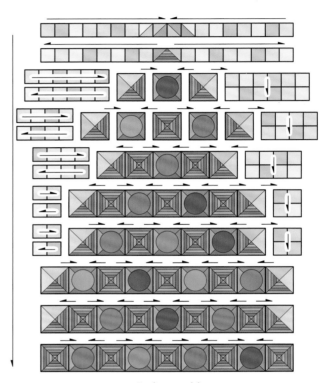

Quilt assembly

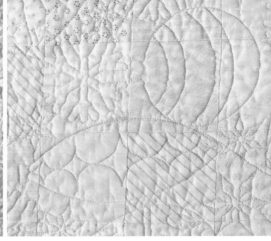

Assembling and Adding the Border

1 Lay out two red floral 3" squares, the red-and-gold half-square-triangle units, and two of the gold half-square-triangle units in two rows as shown. Join the pieces in each row. Join the rows to make the middle portion of the top border strip, which should measure 5½" × 10½", including seam allowances.

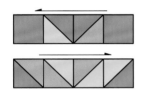

Make 1 unit, 5½" x 10½".

2 Sew together two red floral 5½" × 23" strips and the unit from step 1 to make the top border, which should measure 5½" × 55½", including seam allowances.

Make 1 top border, 5½" x 55½".

3 Join a red-and-green Hourglass block and a red floral 5½" × 40½" strip as shown to make the left border, which should measure 5½" × 45½", including seam allowances.

Make 1 left border, 5½" x 45½".

4 Referring to the diagram, repeat step 3 to make the right border.

Make 1 right border, 5½" x 45½".

5 Sew together two red floral 5½" × 24½" strips, two brown 1½" × 5½" strips, and the brown Hourglass block to make the bottom border, which should measure 5½" × 55½", including seam allowances.

Make 1 bottom border, 5½" x 55½".

6 Sew the left and right borders to the sides of the quilt top, and then add the top and bottom borders. Press all of the seam allowances toward the borders. The completed quilt top should measure 55½" square, including seam allowances.

Finishing the Quilt

Find free, detailed finishing instructions online at ShopMartingale.com/HowtoQuilt.

1 Prepare the quilt backing so it is about 6" larger in both directions than the quilt top.

2 Layer the backing, batting, and quilt top. Baste the layers together.

3 Hand or machine quilt as desired; the quilt shown is machine quilted with an allover design featuring ornament and snowflake shapes.

4 Using the red floral 2½"-wide strips, make the binding and attach it to the quilt.

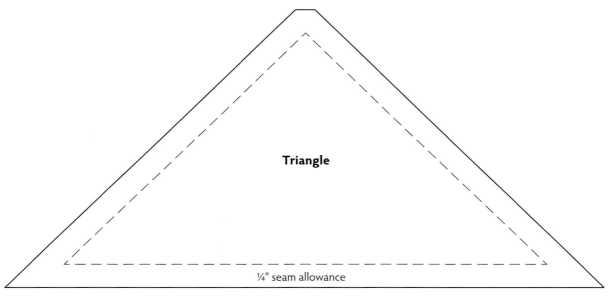

Triangle

¼" seam allowance

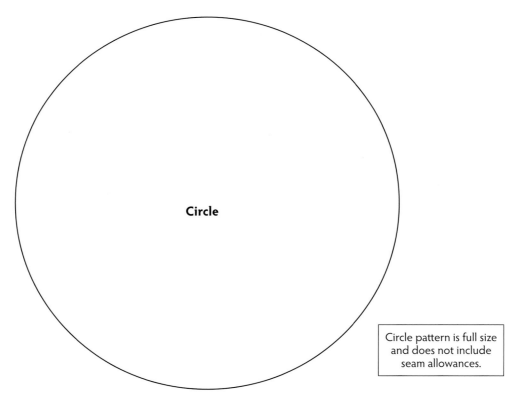

Circle

Circle pattern is full size and does not include seam allowances.

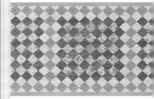

Granny's Gift

QUILT SIZE: 83" × 83" BLOCK SIZE: 10½" × 10½"

 love granny squares, and I wanted to make a granny-square quilt that didn't require me to trim blocks or match up half-square triangles in the setting. Lo and behold, it can be done, and this quilt was a blast to make. Using my favorite red, my go-to neutral, one of my favorite greens, and some pretty low-volume prints for the background, I strip pieced my very own "Granny's Gift."

Materials

Yardage is based on 42"-wide fabric unless otherwise noted. Fat quarters are 18" × 21".

4⅓ yards of cream solid for blocks, side and corner setting triangles, border, and binding*

3⅜ yards of red solid for blocks and side and corner setting triangles*

13 fat quarters of assorted light prints for blocks and side and corner setting triangles

1½ yards of light green solid for blocks and side and corner setting triangles*

⅛ yard of red-and-white gingham for blocks

7⅝ yards of fabric for backing

91" × 91" square of batting

My favorite solids, used here, are all Moda Bella Solids: Persimmon (#294), Ivory (#60), and Pistachio (#134).

Cutting

All measurements include ¼" seam allowances.

From the cream solid, cut:

9 strips, 3½" × 42"

4 strips, 3⅜" × 42"; crosscut into 35 squares, 3⅜" × 3⅜". Cut the squares into quarters diagonally to yield 140 large triangles.

9 strips, 2½" × 42"

36 strips, 2" × 42"; crosscut *15 of the strips* into:
    25 strips, 2" × 20"
    42 squares, 2" × 2"; cut *2 of the squares* in half diagonally to yield 4 small triangles

From the red solid, cut:

55 strips, 2" × 42"; crosscut *44 of the strips* into:
    75 strips, 2" × 20"
    25 strips, 2" × 10"

From *each* of the 13 light print fat quarters, cut:

4 strips, 2" × 20" (52 total; 2 are extra)

4 strips, 2" × 10" (52 total; 2 are extra)

From the light green solid, cut:

23 strips, 2" × 42"; crosscut *7 of the strips* into 116 squares, 2" × 2"

From the red-and-white gingham, cut:

2 strips, 2" × 42"; crosscut into 25 squares, 2" × 2"

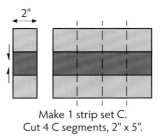

3 Using the same light print as in step 1, sew together two light print strips with one red solid 2" × 10" strip to make strip set C. Crosscut the strip set into four 2"-wide C segments.

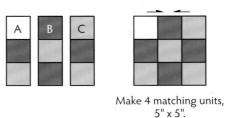

Make 1 strip set C.
Cut 4 C segments, 2" x 5".

4 Sew together one each of segments A, B, and C to make a nine-patch unit. Repeat to make four matching units that measure 5" square, including seam allowances.

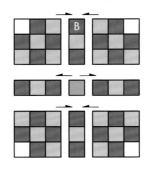

Make 4 matching units,
5" x 5".

5 Lay out the four nine-patch units, four remaining B units, and one red-and-white gingham 2" square in three rows as shown. Sew together the pieces in each row, and then join the rows to make block A, which should measure 11" square, including seam allowances. Repeat steps 1–5 to make 25 A blocks; save all remaining A segments for making B blocks and setting and corner triangles.

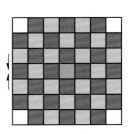

Make 25 A blocks,
11" x 11".

Making the A Blocks

Press the seam allowances as indicated by the arrows.

1 Sew together one cream, one red solid, and one light print 2" × 20" strip as shown to make strip set A. Crosscut the strip set into eight 2"-wide A segments.

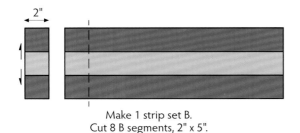

Make 1 strip set A.
Cut 8 A segments, 2" x 5".

2 Using the same light print as in step 1, sew together two red solid strips with one light print 2" × 20" strip as shown to make strip set B. Crosscut the strip set into eight 2"-wide B segments.

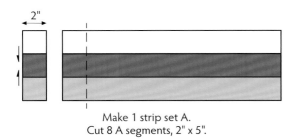

Make 1 strip set B.
Cut 8 B segments, 2" x 5".

So often people pass by blocks like this, where all the squares are set on point. Why? Because each block is bordered by little triangles! Here all the blocks are made from simple Nine Patches, making them effortless to sew and set together. Only the setting triangles around the edges call for triangles. You can do this!

Making the Remaining Units

1 Sew together one green, one cream, and one red solid 2" × 42" strip as shown to make strip set D. Make 11. Crosscut the strip sets into 200 D segments, each 2" wide.

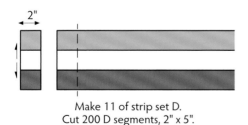

Make 11 of strip set D.
Cut 200 D segments, 2" x 5".

2 Join two cream strips with one green 2" × 42" strip to make strip set E. Make five. Crosscut the strip sets into 80 E segments, each 2" wide.

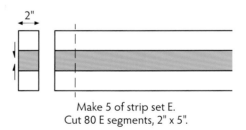

Make 5 of strip set E.
Cut 80 E segments, 2" x 5".

3 Sew together two of segment D and one of segment E as shown to make a nine-patch unit. Repeat to make 80 units that measure 5" square, including seam allowances.

Make 80 units, 5" x 5".

4 Sew together two cream large triangles, two green 2" squares, and one cream 2" square in two vertical rows as shown. Join the rows to make a left unit. Make 20 left units.

Left unit.
Make 20.

5 Using the same pieces in a reverse order and paying attention to orientation, repeat step 4 to make 20 right units.

Right unit.
Make 20.

6 Sew a cream large triangle to one edge of a green 2" square. Add a cream large triangle to the adjacent edge to make a pieced side triangle. Make 16 pieced side triangles.

Side triangle.
Make 16.

7 Sew cream large triangles to opposite edges of a green 2" square and add a cream small triangle to the adjacent side to make a pieced corner triangle. Make four pieced corner triangles.

Corner triangle.
Make 4.

Making the B Blocks and Setting Triangles

1 Before making the B blocks, setting triangles, and corner triangles, you'll need to lay out the A blocks on a design wall so you can match the light print used in the adjacent units. Lay out A blocks in an on-point grid of five blocks by five blocks.

Lay out A blocks.

2 Pin four remaining A segments to each corresponding block on the design wall. When making the units in the following steps, use one A segment from each block that will adjoin the block or setting triangle in the finished quilt.

4 For one side setting triangle, gather one A segment from each of the A blocks next to the space where the setting triangle will be in the finished quilt. Lay out the following units in three vertical rows: a left unit, two D segments, the A segments, a nine-patch unit, a pieced side triangle, and a right unit. Sew together the pieces in each row, and then join the rows to make a side setting triangle. Make 16 side setting triangles and add them to the design wall.

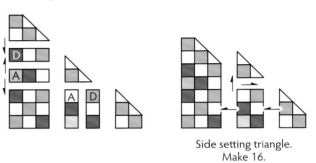

Side setting triangle.
Make 16.

3 For one B block, gather one A segment from each of the A blocks that surround the space where the B block will be in the finished quilt. Lay out the A segments, four nine-patch units, and one green 2" square in three rows as shown. Sew together the pieces in each row, and then join the rows to make block B, which should measure 11" square, including seam allowances. Make 16 B blocks and add them to the design wall.

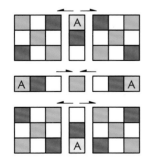
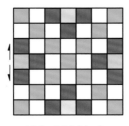

Make 16 B blocks,
11" x 11".

5 Sew together two of segment D and one remaining A segment to make a nine-patch unit. Repeat to make four units that measure 5" square, including seam allowances.

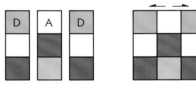

Nine-patch unit.
Make 4 units, 5" x 5".

6 For one corner setting triangle, lay out two cream large triangles and one *each* of a left unit, pieced corner triangle, nine-patch unit from step 5, and right unit as shown. Join the pieces to make a corner triangle. Make four corner setting triangles total and add them to the design wall next to their matching A block.

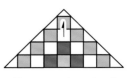

Corner setting triangle.
Make 4.

Assembling the Quilt Top

Referring to the quilt assembly diagram below, add the remaining cream large triangles to each of the indicated setting triangles. Then sew together the pieces in each diagonal row. Join the rows and add the corner setting triangles. The quilt top should measure approximately 77" square, including seam allowances.

Adding the Border

Join the cream 3½" × 42" strips end to end and press the seam allowances open. Trim the pieced length into two 83"-long border strips and two 77"-long border strips. Sew the shorter strips to the sides of the quilt top, and then add the longer strips to the top and bottom edges. The completed quilt top should measure 83" square.

Finishing the Quilt

Find free, detailed finishing instructions online at ShopMartingale.com/HowtoQuilt.

1 Prepare the quilt backing so it is about 8" larger in both directions than the quilt top.

2 Layer the backing, batting, and quilt top. Baste the layers together.

3 Hand or machine quilt as desired; the quilt shown is machine quilted with an allover flower design in the blocks and setting triangles and a braid in the border.

4 Using the cream 2½"-wide strips, make the binding and attach it to the quilt.

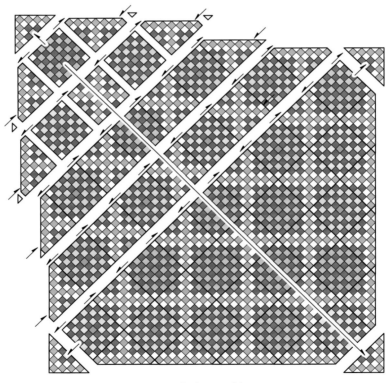

Quilt assembly

Tussy Mussy Christmas

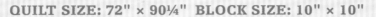

QUILT SIZE: 72" × 90¼" BLOCK SIZE: 10" × 10"

T he Nosegay block is my all-time favorite. I prefer to call it by its alternate name, Tussy Mussy. A tussy mussy, dating back to the Victorian era, is a metal vase specifically designed to be carried. And the word "tus" actually means a "cluster of flowers."

Materials

Yardage is based on 42"-wide fabric. Fat quarters are 18" × 21".

6¼ yards of tan floral for blocks, sashing, setting triangles, inner and outer borders, and binding

½ yard of green floral for blocks

¾ yard of green solid for blocks and middle border

9 fat quarters of assorted red prints for blocks

1⅞ yards of green print for sashing

⅛ yard of red solid for sashing

5½ yards of fabric for backing

80" × 99" piece of batting

Template plastic

Cutting

All measurements include ¼" seam allowances. Trace the kite and triangle patterns on page 39 onto template plastic and cut out the shapes on the drawn lines. Trace the template onto the wrong side of the fabrics specified below, rotating the template 180° after each cut to make the best use of your fabric. Or, see "Susan Says . . ." on page 35 for information on acrylic kite templates.

From the tan floral, cut:

3 squares, 20½" × 20½"; cut the squares into quarters diagonally to yield 12 side setting triangles (you will use 10)

2 squares, 13" × 13"; cut the squares in half diagonally to yield 4 corner setting triangles

2 strips, 3¾" × 42"; crosscut into 18 squares, 3¾" × 3¾". Cut the squares into quarters diagonally to yield 72 small triangles.

9 strips, 3½" × 42"

2 strips, 3⅜" × 42"; crosscut into 18 squares, 3⅜" × 3⅜". Cut the squares in half diagonally to yield 36 large triangles.

17 strips, 2½" × 42"

8 strips, 1¾" × 42"; crosscut *5 of the strips* into 54 rectangles, 1¾" × 3"

22 strips, 1½" × 42"

18 triangles and 18 triangles reversed

From the green floral, cut:

18 kites

Continued on page 34

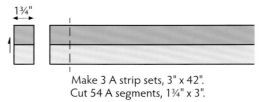

2 Sew together one tan and one green solid 1¾" × 42" strip to make strip set A. Make three A strip sets. From the strip sets, crosscut 54 A segments, each 1¾" wide.

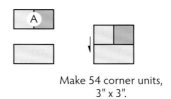

Make 3 A strip sets, 3" x 42".
Cut 54 A segments, 1¾" x 3".

3 Sew an A segment to a tan 1¾" × 3" rectangle to make a corner unit, which should measure 3" square, including seam allowances. Make 54 corner units.

Make 54 corner units,
3" x 3".

4 For one block, gather six large triangles from *each* of two red prints. Join a tan large triangle with one red print large triangle to make a half-square-triangle unit A. It should be 3" square, including seam allowances.

Make 1 of unit A,
3" x 3".

5 Using a large triangle from the other red print, repeat step 4 to make a half-square-triangle unit B. Using one large triangle from each red print, make a half-square-triangle unit C. Make three.

Make 1 of unit B,   Make 3 of unit C,
3" x 3".   3" x 3".

Continued from page 33

From the green solid, cut:

2 strips, 3¾" × 42"; crosscut into 18 squares, 3¾" × 3¾". Cut the squares into quarters diagonally to yield 72 small triangles.

3 strips, 1¾" × 42"

8 strips, 1½" × 42"

From *each* of the 9 assorted red print fat quarters, cut:

12 squares, 3⅜" × 3⅜" (108 total); cut the squares in half diagonally to yield 216 large triangles

From the green print, cut:

39 strips, 1½" × 42"

From the red solid, cut:

2 strips, 1½" × 42"

Making the Blocks

Press the seam allowances as indicated by the arrows.

1 Sew a tan triangle and a reversed triangle to the long edges of a green floral kite piece to make a kite unit, which should measure 5½" square, including seam allowances. Make 18 kite units.

Make 18 kite units,
5½" x 5½".

Susan says...

Coolest. Block. Ever. I love the Tussy Mussy block and it's beautiful in any color combination. While I've included the pattern pieces needed to make templates, I have to tell you I made my version using the BlockLoc 5" kite template set. If you don't mind springing for the templates, you can easily rotary cut and trim your units to perfection. But using the patterns on page 39 will also result in a beautiful quilt. It's good to have options!

6 Lay out one red print large triangle, one tan small triangle, and one green solid triangle. Join the small triangles and add the large triangle to make a bud unit, which should measure 3" square, including seam allowances. Make two matching bud units.

Make 2 bud units,
3" x 3".

7 Using the remaining red print large triangles, repeat step 6 to make two mirror-image bud units as shown.

Make 2 bud units,
3" x 3".

8 Lay out three corner units, all bud units, all half-square-triangle units, and one kite unit in sections as shown. Sew together the units in each horizontal row. Then join the horizontal rows. Sew the joined pieces in the bottom left section to the kite unit and add the top two rows to make a block, which should measure 10½" square, including seam allowances. Repeat steps 4–8 to make 18 blocks total.

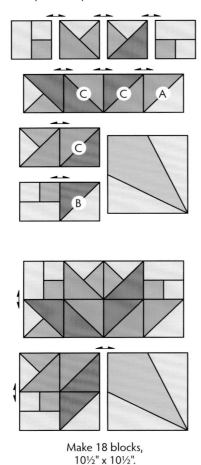

Make 18 blocks,
10½" x 10½".

Making the Sashing Units

1 Sew together one green print and two tan 1½" × 42" strips as shown to make strip set B. Make three. Crosscut the strip sets into 62 B segments, each 1½" wide.

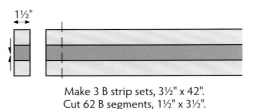

Make 3 B strip sets, 3½" x 42".
Cut 62 B segments, 1½" x 3½".

2 Sew together one red solid and two green print 1½" × 42" strips as shown to make strip set C. Make two. Crosscut the strip sets into 31 C segments, each 1½" wide.

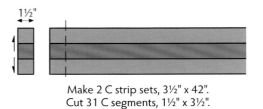

Make 2 C strip sets, 3½" x 42".
Cut 31 C segments, 1½" x 3½".

3 Join two B segments and one C segment to make a nine-patch unit, which should measure 3½" square, including seam allowances. Make 31 nine-patch units.

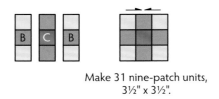

Make 31 nine-patch units,
3½" x 3½".

4 Sew together one tan and two green print 1½" × 42" strips as shown to make strip set D. Make 16 strip sets. Crosscut the strip sets into 48 sashing segments, each 10½" wide.

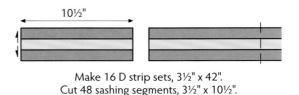

Make 16 D strip sets, 3½" x 42".
Cut 48 sashing segments, 3½" x 10½".

Assembling the Quilt Top

1 Referring to the quilt assembly diagram, lay out the blocks, side and corner setting triangles, nine-patch units, and sashing units in diagonal rows. Note that the setting triangles are oversized and will be trimmed after assembly. Sew together the pieces in each row. Join each block row and its adjacent sashing row as shown. Add the setting or corner triangles to each end of the joined rows. Join the rows and add the corner triangles.

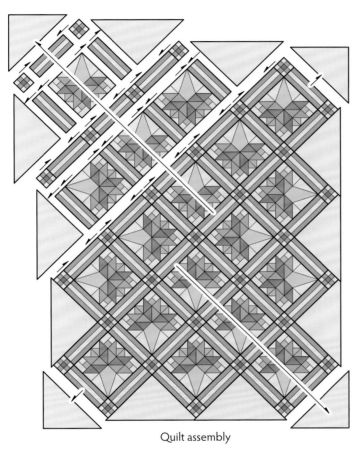

Quilt assembly

Decor Refresh

Popping a pillow on the couch is an easy way to renew a room. You'll find step-by-step instructions for making a coordinating Tussy Mussy Pillow at ShopMartingale.com/CountdowntoChristmas.

Adding the Border

1 Join the tan 2½" × 42" strips end to end and press the seam allowances open. Trim the pieced length into two 78¼"-long inner-border strips and two 64"-long inner-border strips. Sew the longer strips to the sides of the quilt top, and then add the shorter strips to the top and bottom edges. Set the remaining tan strip aside for the binding.

2 Join the remaining green solid 1½" × 42" strips end to end and press the seam allowances open. Trim the pieced length into two 82¼"-long middle-border strips and two 66"-long middle-border strips. Sew the longer strips to the sides of the quilt top, and then add the shorter strips to the top and bottom edges.

3 Join the tan 3½" × 42" strips end to end and press the seam allowances open. Trim the pieced length into two 84¼"-long outer-border strips and two 72"-long outer-border strips. Sew the longer strips to the sides of the quilt top, and then add the shorter strips to the top and bottom edges. The completed quilt top should measure 72" × 90¼", including seam allowances.

2 Carefully trim the excess from the setting triangles, ¼" beyond the points of the nine-patch units. The quilt top should measure 59⅞" × 78¼", including seam allowances.

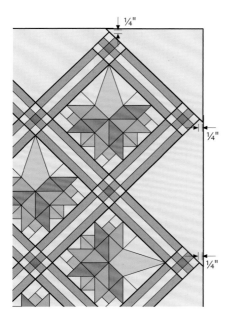

Adding borders

Finishing the Quilt

Find free, detailed finishing instructions online at ShopMartingale.com/HowtoQuilt.

1 Prepare the quilt backing so it is about 8" larger in both directions than the quilt top.

2 Layer the backing, batting, and quilt top. Baste the layers together.

3 Hand or machine quilt as desired; the quilt shown is machine quilted with a feather design in the blocks and setting squares, a braid in the sashing strips, and a braid-and-spiral design in the borders.

4 Using the remaining tan 2½"-wide strips, make the binding and attach it to the quilt.

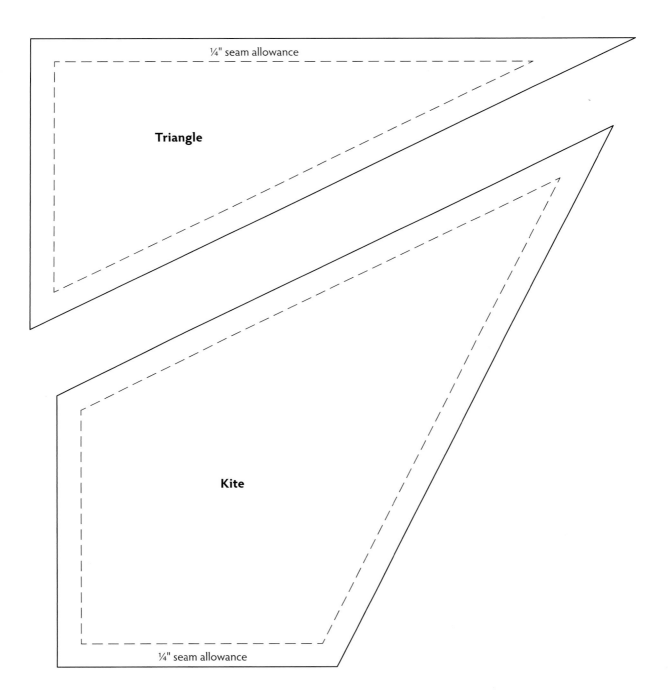

¼" seam allowance

Triangle

Kite

¼" seam allowance

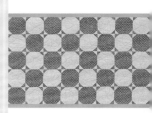

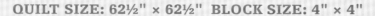

Ho Ho Ho

QUILT SIZE: 62½" × 62½" BLOCK SIZE: 4" × 4"

 hen Moda Fabrics debuted directions for a pieced alphabet called "Spell it with Fabric," I fell crazy in love with piecing words into quilts. If I could find a way to squeeze a word onto a quilt, I did just that. Moda Fabrics said that I could share with you the directions for the letters *H* and *O*. One fun and simple block and two letters will get you a happy holiday HO HO HO!

Materials

Yardage is based on 42"-wide fabric.

3¾ yards of cream solid for blocks, borders, and binding

2½ yards of red print for blocks and middle border

3⅞ yards of fabric for backing

69" × 69" square of batting

Cutting

All measurements include ¼" seam allowances.

From the cream solid, cut:

10 strips, 4½" × 42"; crosscut into:
    10 rectangles, 4½" × 6½"
    10 rectangles, 4½" × 5"
    50 squares, 4½" × 4½"
19 strips, 2½" × 42"; crosscut 5 of the strips into:
    6 strips, 2½" × 10½"
    40 squares, 2½" × 2½"
2 strips, 2" × 42"; crosscut into 4 strips, 2" × 10½"
15 strips, 1½" × 42"; crosscut into:
    2 strips, 1½" × 38½"
    2 strips, 1½" × 36½"
    14 strips, 1½" × 10½"
    164 squares, 1½" × 1½"

From the red print, cut:

6 strips, 4½" × 42"; crosscut into 41 squares, 4½" × 4½"
15 strips, 2½" × 42"; crosscut into:
    20 strips, 2½" × 10½"
    20 strips, 2½" × 8½"
    20 rectangles, 2½" × 6½"
2 strips, 2" × 42"; crosscut into 10 rectangles, 2" × 4½"
7 strips, 1½" × 42"; crosscut into 160 squares, 1½" × 1½"

Making the Blocks

Press the seam allowances as indicated by the arrows.

1 Use a pencil to mark a diagonal line on the wrong side of each cream and red 1½" square.

2 Align a marked cream square right side down on one corner of a red 4½" square as shown. Sew on the drawn line. Trim the seam allowances to ¼" and press the seam allowances toward the red square. Add three more marked squares in the same manner to make an A block, which should measure 4½" square, including seam allowances. Make 41 A blocks.

Make 41 A blocks,
4½" x 4½".

3 Using marked red squares and cream 4½" squares, repeat step 2 to make 40 B blocks; note that the seam allowances are pressed toward the corners, which is the opposite direction as the A blocks.

Make 40 B blocks,
4½" x 4½".

Assembling the Quilt Top

Referring to the quilt assembly diagram, lay out blocks A and B in nine rows of nine blocks each. Sew together the blocks in each row, and then join the rows. The quilt top should measure 36½" square, including seam allowances.

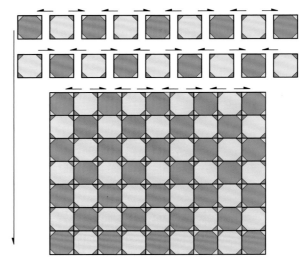

Quilt assembly

Adding the Inner Border

Sew the cream 1½" × 36½" inner-border strips to the sides of the quilt top, and then add the cream 1½" × 38½" inner-border strips to the top and bottom edges. Press the seam allowances toward the border. The quilt top should now measure 38½" square, including seam allowances.

Making the Border Units

1 Use a pencil to mark a diagonal line on the wrong side of each cream 2½" square.

2 Using the same stitch-and-flip method as in "Making the Blocks" on page 42, add a marked square to each end of a red 2½" × 8½" strip to make an O unit. Make 20 O units.

Make 20 O units,
2½" x 8½".

3 Sew together two red 2½" × 6½" strips and one cream 4½" × 6½" rectangle. Add O units to the top and bottom edges to make an O block. Make 10 O blocks, each 8½" × 10½", including seam allowances.

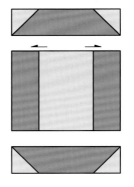

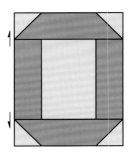

Make 10 O blocks,
8½" x 10½".

4 Sew together one cream 4½" square, one cream 4½" × 5" rectangle, and one red 2" × 4½" rectangle. Sew red 2½" × 10½" strips to the sides of the unit to make an H block. Make 10 H blocks, each 8½" × 10½", including seam allowances.

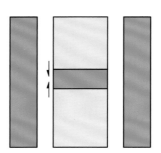
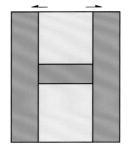

Make 10 H blocks,
8½" x 10½".

Assembling and Adding the Remaining Borders

1 To make a pieced side border, lay out four cream 1½" × 10½" strips, one cream 2½" × 10½" strip, two H blocks, and two O blocks in a row as shown. Join the pieces to make a side border. The pieced border should measure 10½" × 38½", including seam allowances. Repeat to make a second side middle border.

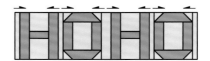

Make 2 side borders,
10½" x 38½".

2 To make the top pieced border, lay out two cream 2" × 10½" strips, three cream 1½" × 10½" strips, two cream 2½" × 10½" strips, three H blocks, and three O blocks in a row. Join the pieces to make the top middle border. The pieced border should measure 10½" × 58½", including seam allowances. Repeat to make the bottom border.

Make 2 top/bottom borders,
10½" x 58½".

3 Sew the side pieced borders to the sides of the quilt top and the top and bottom pieced borders to the top and bottom of the quilt top.

4 Join seven of the remaining cream 2½" × 42" strips end to end and press the seam allowances open. Trim the pieced length into two 62½"-long outer-border strips and two 58½"-long outer-border strips. Sew the shorter strips to the sides of the quilt

top, and then add the longer strips to the top and bottom. The completed quilt top should measure 62½" square.

Finishing the Quilt

Find free, detailed finishing instructions online at ShopMartingale.com/HowtoQuilt.

1 Prepare the quilt backing so it is about 6" larger in both directions than the quilt top.

2 Layer the backing, batting, and quilt top. Baste the layers together.

3 Hand or machine quilt as desired; the quilt shown is machine quilted with an allover design of interlocking curved triangles in the quilt center. The inner and middle borders were quilted with wavy lines radiating out from the quilt center, and the outer border was stitched with a snowflake motif.

4 Using the seven remaining cream 2½"-wide strips, make the binding and attach it to the quilt.

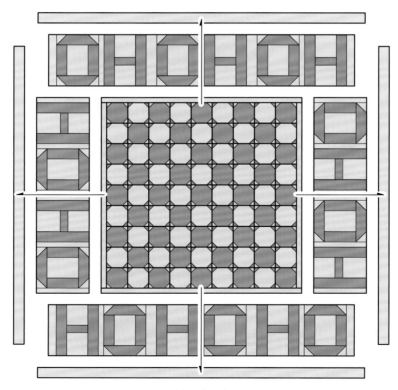

Adding borders

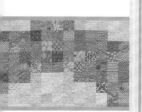
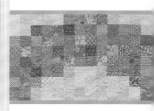

Christmas Welcome

QUILT SIZE: 44½" × 44½"

othing says "welcome" at the holidays like the fresh evergreen wreath hanging on my front door. Even with the sun beating down and the tips of the greenery turning a bit brown in the Florida weather, the aroma of fresh greenery is my favorite kind of welcome every single year. The bows may change year to year, but the evergreen will always be your first hello to my holiday home.

Materials

Yardage is based on 42"-wide fabric unless otherwise noted. Fat eighths are 9" × 21".

10 fat eighths of assorted light prints for quilt background
8 to 10 fat eighths of assorted green prints for wreath
¾ yard of red tone on tone for inner border and bow
1 yard of multicolored floral for outer border and binding
2⅞ yards of fabric for backing
51" × 51" square of batting

Cutting

All measurements include ¼" seam allowances.

From the assorted light fat eighths, cut:
40 strips, 2" × 21"; crosscut *8 of the strips* into 64 squares, 2" × 2"

From the assorted green fat eighths, cut:
30 strips, 2" × 21", crosscut *2 of the strips* into 12 squares, 2" × 2"

From the red tone on tone, cut:
1 strip, 6½" × 40"
1 rectangle, 10" × 18½"
5 strips, 1½" × 42"; crosscut *1 of the strips* into 4 rectangles, 1½" × 3½" (save the leftover part of the strip for piecing the inner border)

From the multicolored floral, cut:
5 strips, 3½" × 42"; crosscut into:
    4 strips, 3½" × 36½"
    4 squares, 3½" × 3½"
5 strips, 2½" × 42"

With or Without

While a big red bow is a perfect finishing touch on a wreath, if you leave off the bow, this quilt does double duty as a lovely table topper with space to display a special centerpiece.

Making the Blocks

Press the seam allowances as indicated by the arrows.

1 Sew together five assorted light 2" × 21" strips as shown to make strip set A. Make four strip sets. Crosscut the strip sets into 32 A segments, each 2" wide.

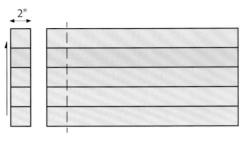

Make 4 A strip sets, 8" x 21".
Cut 32 A segments.

2 Sew together four assorted light 2" × 21" strips as shown to make strip set B. Make three strip sets. Crosscut the strip sets into 24 B segments, each 2" wide.

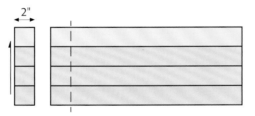

Make 3 B strip sets, 6½" x 21".
Cut 24 B segments.

3 Sew together five assorted green 2" × 21" strips as shown to make strip set C. Make four strip sets. Crosscut the strip sets into 36 C segments, each 2" wide.

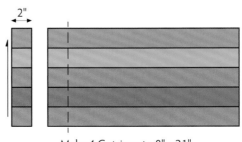

Make 4 C strip sets, 8" x 21".
Cut 36 C segments.

4 Sew together four assorted green 2" × 21" strips as shown to make strip set D. Make two strip sets. Crosscut the strip sets into 16 D segments, each 2" wide.

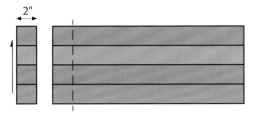

Make 2 D strip sets, 6½" x 21".
Cut 16 D segments.

Assembling the Quilt Top

Referring to the quilt assembly diagram below, lay out segments A–D, the assorted light 2" squares, and assorted green 2" squares in 24 horizontal rows. (The bottom 12 rows are a mirror image of the top 12 rows.) Position the segments so their seam allowances are pressed in the same direction as the finished rows will be pressed. Sew together the pieces in each row. Join the rows. Press the seam allowances toward the bottom of the quilt. The quilt top should measure 36½" square, including seam allowances.

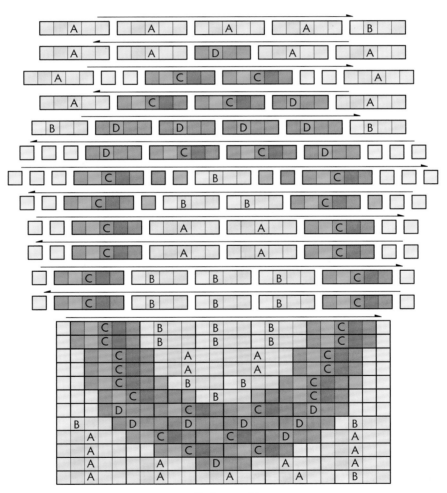

Quilt assembly

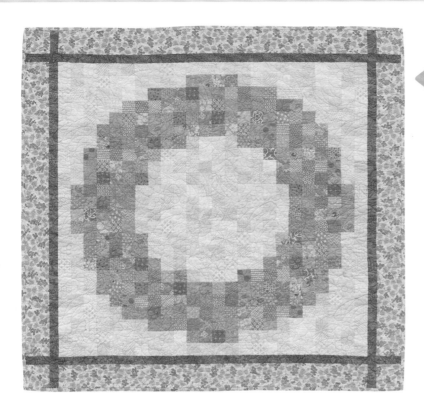

Adding the Borders

1 Join two multicolored floral 3½" squares, two red 1½" × 3½" rectangles, and one multicolored floral 3½" × 36½" strip to make the top outer border, which should measure 3½" × 44½", including seam allowances. Repeat to make the bottom outer border.

Make 2 top/bottom borders, 3½" x 44½".

2 Join the red 1½ × 42" strips end to end and press the seam allowances open. Trim the pieced length into two 44½"-long inner-border strips and two 36½"-long inner-border strips.

3 Sew the shorter inner-border strips to the sides of the quilt top. Sew red 1½" × 3½" rectangles to each end of the multicolored floral 3½" × 36½" outer-border strips; sew these strips to the sides of the quilt top. Press the seam allowances toward the outer border. Sew the remaining inner-border strips to the top and bottom edges of the quilt. Then add the pieced outer-border strips to the top and bottom edges. Press the seam allowances toward the outer border. The completed quilt top should measure 44½" square, including seam allowances.

Finishing the Quilt

Find free, detailed finishing instructions online at ShopMartingale.com/HowtoQuilt.

1 Prepare the quilt backing so it is about 6" larger in both directions than the quilt top.

2 Layer the backing, batting, and quilt top. Baste the layers together.

3 Hand or machine quilt as desired; the quilt shown is machine quilted with an allover design of ribbon candy and snowflakes.

4 Using the multicolored 2½"-wide strips, make the binding and attach it to the quilt.

Making the Bow

1 Fold the red 6½" × 40" strip in half lengthwise with right sides together. Leaving an opening for turning in the middle of the strip, sew the long edges together. At each end of the strip, mark and sew a line at a 45° angle from the fold to the previous seam. Trim the seam allowances close to the stitching at the points, then turn right side out. This will be the tie. Press flat. Hand or machine stitch the opening closed.

Leave open.

45°   45°

2 Fold the red 10" × 18½" rectangle in half lengthwise with right sides together. Sew the long edges together.

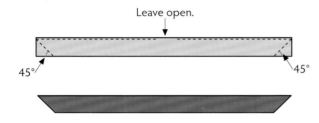

3 Turn the tube right side out and press flat. Fold the tube in half widthwise and sew the ends together. Press the seam allowances open, turn so the seam allowances are on the inside, and center them in the back of the tube. This will be the bow.

 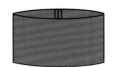

4 Pleat the center of the bow a few times and hold in place by wrapping several times with doubled thread; tie thread ends in a knot. Fold the center of the tie in half, place it over the center of the bow, and tie in place on the back of the bow.

5 Pull both tie ends down and arrange them as desired, tacking with a few stitches if necessary to get them to stay where you want them. Hand-tack or pin to the wreath quilt. You may wish to take the bow off and store it separately from the quilt when the quilt is not on display.

Tree Farming

QUILT SIZE: 63½" × 78½"   BLOCK SIZE: 3⅝" × 10"

When the idea for this tree quilt came to me, I pulled out every single green that was in the scrap pile. I wanted the quilt to be a super-colorful version of a tree farm. When lots of one color is featured in a quilt, to me there is no right or wrong shade of that color. Playing with scrap colors is also a great way for me to fall in love all over again with fabric I may not have touched for ages.

Materials

Yardage is based on 42"-wide fabric.

4⅜ yards *total* of assorted light prints for blocks
   and outer border
2⅞ yards *total* of assorted green prints for blocks
   and outer border
⅓ yard *total* of assorted brown prints for blocks
1 yard of red gingham for inner border and binding
4⅞ yards of fabric for backing
72" × 87" piece of batting
Template plastic

Cutting

All measurements include ¼" seam allowances. Trace the triangle A and B patterns on page 57 onto template plastic and cut out the shapes on the drawn lines. Trace the templates onto the wrong side of the fabrics specified below, rotating the templates 180° after each cut to make the best use of your fabric.

From the light prints, cut *105 sets* of:
2 squares, 1½" × 1½"
1 rectangle, 1½" × 4⅛"
1 *each* of A and A reversed

From the remaining light prints, cut a *total* of:
45 squares, 3½" × 3½"
180 squares, 1½" × 1½"

From the green prints, cut a *total* of:
45 squares, 3½" × 3½"
180 squares, 1½" × 1½"
105 of B

From the brown prints, cut a *total* of:
105 rectangles, 1½" × 2⅛"

From the red gingham, cut:
4 strips, 1⅞" × 42"
3 strips, 1½" × 42"
300" total of 2½"-wide bias strips

Susan says...

Don't be intimidated by the long skinny trees. There are no places in this quilt where points meet other points, so you don't have to worry about chopping the tops off your trees! Besides, everyone will be so busy looking at your fabulous collection of green prints that no one will notice if any of the points aren't perfect.

Making the Blocks

Press the seam allowances as indicated by the arrows.

1 Sew together a light A triangle and a green B triangle. Add a matching A reversed triangle as shown to make a tree unit. Make 105 tree units.

Make 105 tree units,
4⅛" x 8½".

2 Join two matching light 1½" squares and a brown 1½" × 2⅛" rectangle as shown to make a trunk unit. Make 105 trunk units.

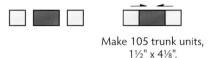

Make 105 trunk units, 1½" x 4⅛".

3 Matching the light print, sew a tree unit to a trunk unit. Make 105 units.

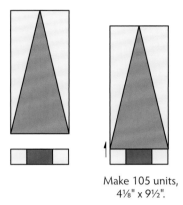

Make 105 units, 4⅛" x 9½".

4 Sew a matching light print 1½" × 4⅛" rectangle to the top edge of a unit from step 3 to make a Tree block, which should measure 4⅛" × 10½", including seam allowances. Make 56 of these blocks. Add the light print rectangle to the bottom edge of the remaining 49 units to make 49 blocks.

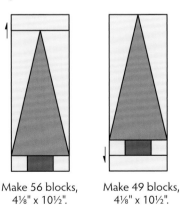

Make 56 blocks, 4⅛" x 10½".   Make 49 blocks, 4⅛" x 10½".

Assembling the Quilt Top

Referring to the quilt assembly diagram above right, lay out the blocks in seven rows of 15 blocks each (eight with the light rectangle on top and seven with the light rectangle on bottom). Sew together the blocks in each row. Join the rows. The quilt top should measure 55" × 70½", including seam allowances.

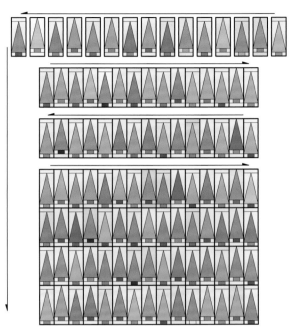

Quilt assembly

Adding the Border

1 Use a pencil to mark a diagonal line on the wrong side of each green and light 1½" square.

2 Align a marked green square right sides together on one corner of a light 3½" square as shown. Sew on the drawn line. Trim the seam allowances to ¼" and press the resulting triangle toward the corner. Add three more marked squares in the same manner to make a light Snowball block, which should measure 3½" square, including seam allowances. Make 45 light Snowball blocks.

Make 45 light Snowball blocks, 3½" x 3½".

3 In the same manner, use four marked light 1½" squares and one green 3½" square to make a dark Snowball block; note that the seam allowances are pressed in the opposite direction as the light blocks. Make 45 dark Snowball blocks.

Make 45 dark
Snowball blocks,
3½" x 3½".

4 Join the red gingham 1⅞" × 42" strips end to end and press the seam allowances open. Trim the pieced length into two 70½"-long inner-border strips. Sew these strips to the side edges of the quilt. Join the red gingham 1½" × 42" strips end to end and press the seam allowances open. Trim the pieced length into two 57½"-long inner-border strips. Add these strips to the top and bottom edges. Press the seam allowances toward the inner border.

5 Sew together 12 dark and 12 light Snowball blocks, alternating dark and light blocks, to make a side outer border. Make two side outer borders.

Make 2 side outer borders, 3½" x 72½".

6 Join 11 dark and 10 light Snowball blocks, alternating them as shown to make the top outer border. Sew together 11 light and 10 dark Snowball blocks as shown to make the bottom outer border.

Make 1 top outer border, 3½" x 63½".

Make 1 bottom outer border, 3½" x 63½".

7 Sew the side outer borders to the quilt top with the light Snowball blocks at the top. Add the top and bottom outer borders to complete the quilt top, which should measure 63½" × 78½", including seam allowances. Press the seam allowances toward the inner border.

Finishing the Quilt

Find free, detailed finishing instructions online at ShopMartingale.com/HowtoQuilt.

1 Prepare the quilt backing so it is about 6" larger in both directions than the quilt top.

2 Layer the backing, batting, and quilt top. Baste the layers together.

3 Hand or machine quilt as desired; the quilt shown is machine quilted with an allover leaf-and-spiral design in the quilt center. Each Snowball block in the outer border was stitched with a spiral, leaf, or tree motif.

4 Using the red gingham 2½"-wide strips, make the binding and attach it to the quilt.

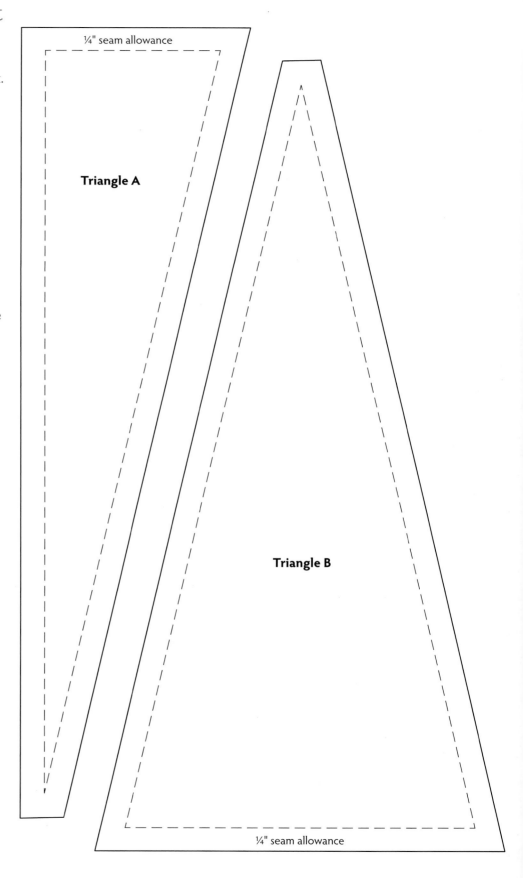

¼" seam allowance

Triangle A

Triangle B

¼" seam allowance

Peppermint Party

QUILT SIZE: 75½" × 75½"   BLOCK SIZE: 9" × 9"

fficially, my countdown to Christmas begins when the stores start stocking all kinds of peppermint bark. Suddenly, it seems as though my entire day involves eating some sort of peppermint sweet, and this will continue until the last of my Christmas decorations have been taken down. When the stores bring out their peppermint treats is also when I take out all of my red-and-white quilts to stack, hang, and drape all over the house.

Materials

Yardage is based on 42"-wide fabric. Fat quarters are 18" × 21".

½ yard of dark red tone on tone for block A corners

9 fat quarters of assorted light prints for blocks

9 fat quarters of assorted red prints for blocks

⅜ yard of red gingham for block B corners

2½ yards of cream tone on tone for block borders, outer border, and binding

1½ yards of white solid for sashing and inner border

1⅓ yards of red-and-white polka dot for sashing and inner border

7 yards of fabric for backing

84" × 84" square of batting

Template plastic

Cutting

All measurements include ¼" seam allowances. Trace the triangle pattern on page 64 onto template plastic and cut out the shape on the drawn lines. Trace the template onto the wrong side of the 5⅜"-wide strips specified below, rotating the template 180° after each cut to make the best use of your fabric.

From the dark red tone on tone, cut:

4 strips, 3½" × 42"; crosscut the strips into 40 squares, 3½" × 3½". Cut the squares in half diagonally to yield 80 corner triangles.

From *each* of the 9 assorted light print fat quarters, cut:

3 strips, 5⅜" × 21" (27 total). From each set of 3 strips, cut 16 triangles (144 total)

From *each* of the 9 assorted red print fat quarters, cut:

3 strips, 5⅜" × 21" (27 total). From each set of 3 strips, cut 16 triangles (144 total)

From the red gingham, cut:

3 strips, 3½" × 42"; crosscut the strips into 32 squares, 3½" × 3½". Cut the squares in half diagonally to yield 64 corner triangles.

From the cream tone on tone, cut:

8 strips, 3½" × 42"

8 strips, 2½" × 42"

8 strips, 2" × 30½"

8 strips, 2" × 27½"

Continued on page 60

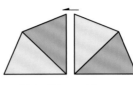

2 Join two matching quarter units to make a half unit. Make 72 total (36 pairs of matching half units). Sew together two half units to make a block unit. Make 36 block units.

Make 36 matching sets of 2 (72 total).

Make 36.

Continued from page 59

From the white solid, cut:

1 strip, 3⅞" × 42"; crosscut into 4 squares, 3⅞" × 3⅞"

12 strips, 3½" × 42"; crosscut into 122 squares, 3½" × 3½"

From the red-and-white polka dot, cut:

1 strip, 3⅞" × 42"; crosscut into 4 squares, 3⅞" × 3⅞"

11 strips, 3½" × 42"; crosscut into 61 rectangles, 3½" × 6½"

Making the Blocks

Press the seam allowances as indicated by the arrows.

1 Sew together a light and a red triangle from the triangle pattern to make a quarter unit. Make 144 (36 sets of four matching quarter units).

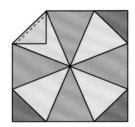
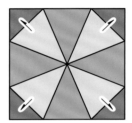

3 Sew four dark red corner triangles to the light print triangles to make block A. Make 20 A blocks, each 9½" square, including seam allowances.

Make 20 A blocks, 9½" x 9½".

4 Using red gingham corner triangles and sewing them to the red print triangles, repeat step 4 to make block B. Make 16 B blocks.

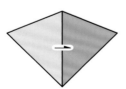

Quarter unit.
Make 36 matching sets of 4 (144 total).

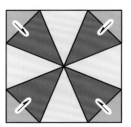

Make 16 B blocks, 9½" x 9½".

5 Lay out five A blocks and four B blocks in three rows as shown. Sew together the blocks in each row, and then join the rows to complete a nine-block unit, which should be 27½" square, including seam allowances. Make four nine-block units.

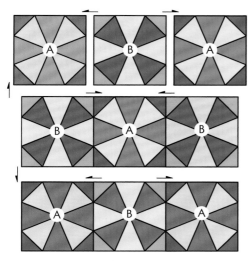

Make 4 units,
27½" x 27½".

6 Sew cream tone-on-tone 2" × 27½" strips to two sides of a nine-block unit. Then add cream tone-on-tone 2" × 30½" strips to the remaining sides. The bordered nine-block unit should measure 30½" square, including seam allowances. Make four bordered nine-block units.

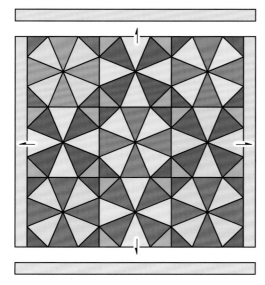

Make 4 units,
30½" x 30½".

Making the Sashing and Border Units

1 Use a pencil to mark a diagonal line on the wrong side of each white solid 3½" square and 3⅞" square.

2 Align a marked 3½" square right sides together on one end of a red-and-white polka dot 3½" × 6½" rectangle as shown. Sew on the drawn line. Trim the seam allowances to ¼" and press the resulting triangle toward the corner. Add a second marked square to the remaining end of the rectangle as shown to make a sashing unit. Make 31 sashing units, 3½" × 6½", including seam allowances. Rotating the direction of the marked line on the squares, make 30 mirror-image sashing units.

 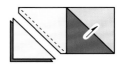

Make 31 sashing units,
3½" x 6½".

Make 30 sashing units,
3½" x 6½".

3 Place a marked 3⅞" square right sides together with a red-and-white polka dot 3⅞" square. Sew ¼" from each side of the marked line. Cut apart on the marked line and press open to make two half-square-triangle units, each 3½" square, including seam allowances. Make eight half-square-triangle units (you will use seven).

Make 8 half-square-triangle units,
3½" x 3½".

I love all things peppermint, but I'm not a huge fan of having to match a lot of triangle intersections. That's why I divided the blocks in this quilt top with candy-cane-striped sashing. If all four of the big blocks were joined without sashing, the quilt would be lovely—but who needs that stress while preparing for the holidays?

Assembling the Quilt Top

1 Referring to the diagram at right, sew together four sashing units and two half-square-triangle units to make a horizontal sashing strip, 3½" × 30½", including seam allowances. Join five sashing units to make a second horizontal sashing strip, 3½" × 30½", including seam allowances. Sew together one half-square-triangle unit and 10 mirror-image sashing units to make a vertical sashing/side inner-border strip. Make three, each 3½" × 63½", including seam allowances. Join one half-square-triangle unit and

11 sashing units to make a top/bottom inner-border strip. Make two, each 3½" × 69½", including seam allowances.

Horizontal sashing. Make 1 of each.

Vertical sashing and side borders. Make 3.

Top/bottom borders. Make 2.

2 Referring to the quilt assembly diagram below, sew together the four bordered nine-block units, the horizontal sashing strips, and the vertical sashing strip in vertical rows. Join the block and sashing rows to make the quilt center, which should measure 63½" square, including seam allowances.

3 Sew the side inner-border strips to the sides of the quilt center. Add the top/bottom inner-border strips to the top and bottom edges of the quilt center.

4 Join the cream tone-on-tone 3½" × 42" strips end to end and press the seam allowances open. Trim the pieced length into two 69½"-long outer-border strips and two 75½"-long outer-border strips. Sew the shorter strips to the sides of the quilt top, and then add the longer strips to the top and bottom edges. The completed quilt top should measure 75½" square, including seam allowances.

Finishing the Quilt

Find free, detailed finishing instructions online at ShopMartingale.com/HowtoQuilt.

1 Prepare the quilt backing so it is about 8" larger in both directions than the quilt top.

2 Layer the backing, batting, and quilt top. Baste the layers together.

3 Hand or machine quilt as desired; the quilt shown is machine quilted with an allover spiral-and-circle design.

4 Using the cream tone-on-tone 2½"-wide strips, make the binding and attach it to the quilt.

Quilt assembly

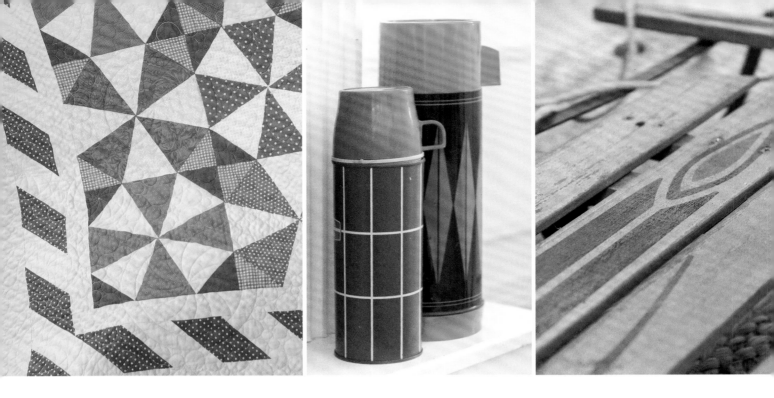

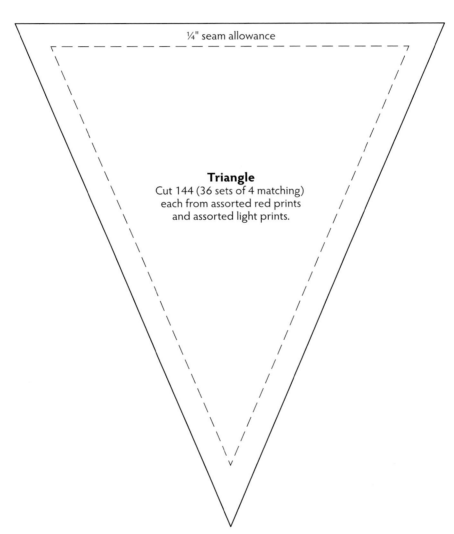

¼" seam allowance

Triangle
Cut 144 (36 sets of 4 matching)
each from assorted red prints
and assorted light prints.

Tiddlywinks

QUILT SIZE: 80½" × 80½"   BLOCK SIZE: 21" × 21"

henever I hear the statement, "but it's just a gentle curve," I think to myself, "Well, it may seem that way to you, but it certainly looks like the Daytona 500 curved speedway to me!" But there are tons of tutorials and videos on how to piece a gentle curve. So I jumped right in after watching them. I finger-pressed the center on both pieces and pinned them together. I was able to make stacks of pinned pieces, and then I sat down to sew them all at once. This is my grand hint for curved piecing—just start piecing them. Don't worry too much about perfection, because once you get a sewing rhythm going, you'll notice that it isn't as difficult as your mind was making it out to be. My go-to Bella Solid Ivory #60 and the very beautiful Bella Solid Chartreuse #188 were just the colors I needed for this fun way to play with curves.

Materials

Yardage is based on 42"-wide fabric.

5⅝ yards of green solid for blocks, inner border, outer border, and binding

3⅞ yards of ivory solid for blocks and middle border

7½ yards of fabric for backing

89" × 89" square of batting

Template plastic

Cutting

All measurements include ¼" seam allowances. Trace patterns A and B on page 69 onto template plastic and cut out the shapes on the drawn lines. Trace the templates onto the wrong side of the fabrics specified below and cut out. Be sure to transfer the center marks and corner matching points to the templates and then to the fabric pieces. These are used when joining the pieces.

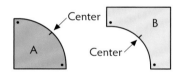

From the green solid, cut:

7 strips, 4" × 42"

8 strips, 3½" × 42"

9 strips, 2½" × 42"

144 of A

180 of B

From the ivory solid, cut:

8 strips, 2½" × 42"

180 of A

144 of B

Making the Blocks

Press the seam allowances as indicated by the arrows.

1 With right sides together, match the center points of a green A piece and an ivory B piece; pin in place with a slender pin, picking up just a few threads of the fabric. Repeat to pin the pieces together at the dots at each end of the curve. Sew together along the curved edge, slowly easing the fabrics to fit (you can clip into the curve of the ivory piece if necessary to make the seam lines fit together). The light unit should measure 4" square including seam allowances. Make 144 light units.

Make 144 light units,
4" x 4".

2 Using ivory A pieces and green B pieces, make 180 dark units.

Make 180 dark units,
4" x 4".

3 Lay out 16 light units and 20 dark units in six rows as shown. Sew together the units in each row. Join the rows to make a block, which should measure 21½" square, including seam allowances. Make nine blocks.

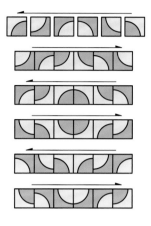

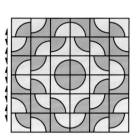

Make 9 blocks,
21½" x 21½".

Assembling the Quilt Top

Referring to the quilt assembly diagram, lay out the blocks in three rows of three blocks each. Sew together the blocks in each row. Join the rows. The quilt top should measure 63½" square, including seam allowances.

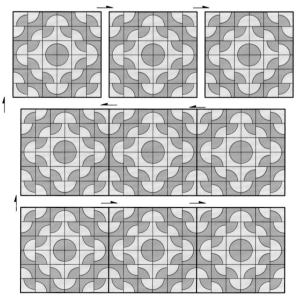

Quilt assembly

Adding the Borders

1 Join the green 4" x 42" strips end to end and press the seam allowances open. Trim the pieced length into two 70½"-long inner-border strips and two 63½"-long inner-border strips.

2 Join the ivory 2½" × 42" strips end to end and press the seam allowances open. Trim the pieced length into two 74½"-long middle-border strips and two 70½"-long middle-border strips.

3 Join the green 3½" × 42" strips end to end and press the seam allowances open. Trim the pieced length into two 80½"-long outer-border strips and two 74½"-long outer-border strips.

4 Sew the shorter inner-border strips to the sides of the quilt top; then add the longer strips to the top and bottom edges. Press the seam allowances toward the inner border. Repeat to add the middle- and outer-border strips. The completed quilt top should measure 80½" square.

Finishing the Quilt

Find free, detailed finishing instructions online at ShopMartingale.com/HowtoQuilt.

1 Prepare the quilt backing so it is about 8" larger in both directions than the quilt top.

2 Layer the backing, batting, and quilt top. Baste the layers together.

3 Hand or machine quilt as desired; the quilt shown is machine quilted with an allover spiral-and-feather design in the quilt center and diagonal parallel lines in the borders.

4 Using the green 2½"-wide strips, make the binding and attach it to the quilt.

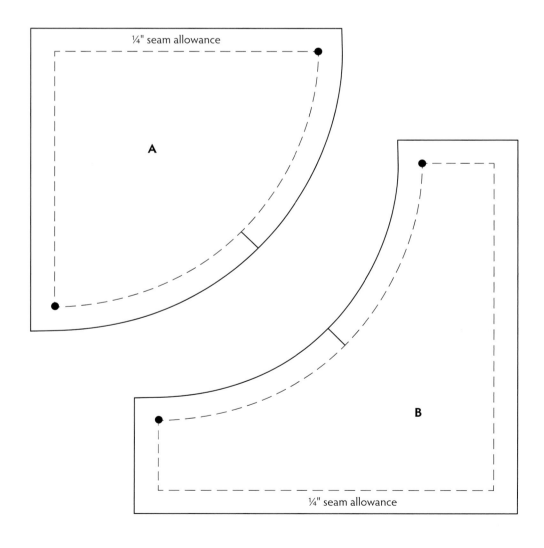

¼" seam allowance

A

¼" seam allowance

B

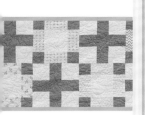
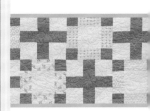

Background Music

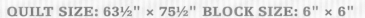

QUILT SIZE: 63½" × 75½" BLOCK SIZE: 6" × 6"

 Often in a quilt, the colors take center stage. Well, this is one time I wanted backgrounds to be the star of the show. All of those great red-and-white background prints you've collected, it's time to use them for a perfect calm holiday quilt. This is such a fun quilt to reimagine—larger, smaller, borders, no borders—because the two blocks are a simple repeat. I wanted a good lap size to snuggle up in to watch holiday movies, but don't let that influence where you might use yours. Maybe make a tablecloth, a guest quilt, a great gift, or just some blocks for a fun pillow.

Materials

Yardage is based on 42"-wide fabric. Fat eighths are 9" × 21".

17 fat eighths of assorted light prints for A blocks
2⅛ yards of light red solid for blocks, border, and
    border corner blocks
3¼ yards of cream solid for blocks, border,
    border corner blocks, and binding
4⅝ yards of fabric for backing
70" × 82" piece of batting

Cutting

All measurements include ¼" seam allowances.

From *each* of the 17 light print fat eighths, cut:
3 strips, 2" × 21" (51 total); crosscut into 12
    rectangles, 2" × 3½" (204 total; 4 will be extra)

From the light red solid, cut:
34 strips, 2" × 42"; crosscut 20 of the strips into:
    2 strips, 2" × 20"
    1 strip, 2" × 10"
    49 rectangles, 2" × 6½"
    200 squares, 2" × 2"

From the cream solid, cut:
5 strips, 3½" × 42"; crosscut into 50 squares,
    3½" × 3½"
14 strips, 2¾ " × 42"
8 strips, 2½" × 42"
15 strips, 2" × 42"; crosscut 1 of the strips into:
    1 strip, 2" × 20"
    2 strips, 2" × 10"

> ### Playing Favorites
>
> Do you have a favorite red solid? Moda Bella Solid Persimmon #294 is mine, and it's my go-to for all projects that include a red solid.

Susan says...

Did you notice the super-cute pillow in the basket on page 70? It's simply a smaller version of this lap quilt! Sew four A and five B blocks together into a big Nine Patch, and you've got the makings of an 18" pillow! Pair it with this lap-sized quilt, and you'll be ready to binge-watch an entire season of holiday movies. Find step-by-step instructions for the Background Music Pillow at ShopMartingale.com /CountdowntoChristmas.

Making the Blocks

Press the seam allowances as indicated by the arrows.

1 Lay out four red 2" squares, four matching light 2" × 3½" rectangles, and one cream 3½" square in three rows as shown. Sew together the pieces in each row, and then join the rows to make block A. Make 50 A blocks, each 6½" square, including seam allowances.

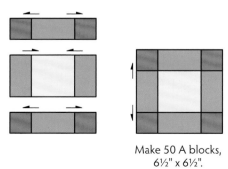

Make 50 A blocks, 6½" x 6½".

2 Sew together two cream 2¾" × 42" strips and one red 2" × 42" strip to make strip set A. Make seven. Crosscut the strip sets into 98 A segments, each 2¾" wide.

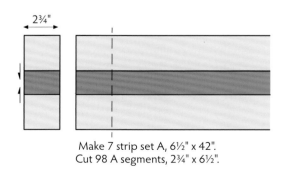

Make 7 strip set A, 6½" x 42".
Cut 98 A segments, 2¾" x 6½".

3 Join two A segments and one red 2" × 6½" rectangle to make block B. Make 49 B blocks, each 6½" square, including seam allowances.

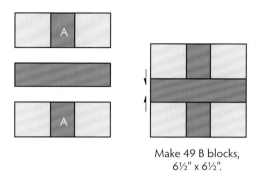

Make 49 B blocks, 6½" x 6½".

Assembling the Quilt Top

Referring to the quilt assembly diagram below, lay out blocks A and B in 11 rows of nine blocks each. Join the blocks in each row, and then join the rows. The quilt top should measure 54½" × 66½", including seam allowances.

Making and Adding the Border

1 Sew together two red 2" × 20" strips and one cream 2" × 20" strip as shown to make strip set B. Crosscut the strip set into eight B segments, each 2" wide.

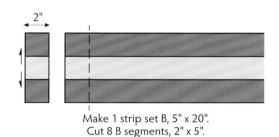

Make 1 strip set B, 5" x 20".
Cut 8 B segments, 2" x 5".

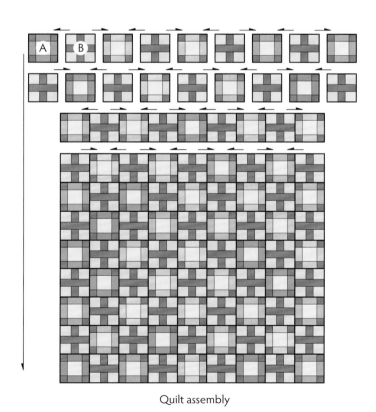

Quilt assembly

5 Sew together one red and two cream 66½"-long strips to make a side border. Make two side borders.

Make 2 side borders, 5" x 66½".

6 Sew together one red and two cream 54½"-long strips. Add a nine-patch unit to each end of the joined strips to make the top border. Repeat to make the bottom border.

Make 2 top/bottom borders, 5" x 63½".

7 Sew the side borders to the sides of the quilt top, and then add the top and bottom borders. The completed quilt top should measure 63½" × 75½", including seam allowances.

Finishing the Quilt

Find free, detailed finishing instructions online at ShopMartingale.com/HowtoQuilt.

1 Prepare the quilt backing so it is about 6" larger in both directions than the quilt top.

2 Layer the backing, batting, and quilt top. Baste the layers together.

3 Hand or machine quilt as desired; the quilt shown is machine quilted with an allover holly leaf and berry design in the blocks and a loop in the border.

4 Using the cream 2½"-wide strips, make the binding and attach it to the quilt.

2 Sew together two cream 2" × 10" strips and one red 2" × 10" strip as shown to make strip set C. Crosscut the strip set into four C segments, each 2" wide.

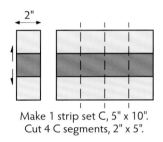

Make 1 strip set C, 5" x 10".
Cut 4 C segments, 2" x 5".

3 Sew together two B segments and one C segment as shown to make a nine-patch unit. Make four units that measure 5" square, including seam allowances.

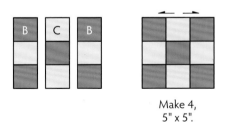

Make 4,
5" x 5".

4 Join the remaining cream 2" × 42" strips end to end and press the seam allowances open. Trim the pieced length into four 66½"-long strips and four 54½"-long strips. Join the remaining red 2" × 42" strips end to end and press the seam allowances open. Trim the pieced length into two 66½"-long strips and two 54½"-long strips.

Crisscross Applesauce

QUILT SIZE: 76½" × 76½" BLOCK SIZE: 9¾" × 9¾"

Besides being fun to say, Crisscross Applesauce is fun to make. Combine your happiest greens and reds, and suddenly the Christmas season is ready to begin. There was a plan in the beginning, and it started with picking one of my favorite red prints for the border, a pretty green that wasn't too busy for my sashing, and a tan background I just knew had to play a part in this quilt. By that time, the quilt was scrappy enough that there were no "wrong" combinations of red and green for the stars.

Materials

Yardage is based on 42"-wide fabric. Fat quarters are 18" × 21".

12 strips, 2½" × 42", of assorted red prints for blocks
12 strips, 2½" × 42", of assorted green prints for blocks
12 fat quarters of assorted white prints for block backgrounds
2 yards of green floral for sashing
¼ yard of red solid for sashing
1 yard of tan print for setting triangles
1⅞ yards of red floral for border and binding
7⅛ yards of fabric for backing
85" × 85" square of batting
Acrylic ruler with 45° marking

Cutting

All measurements include ¼" seam allowances.

From *each* of the red and green prints, cut:
2 strips, 2½" × 20" (24 red and 24 green total)

From *each* of the 12 white print fat quarters, cut:
8 squares, 3¾" × 3¾"; cut the squares in half diagonally to yield 16 large triangles (192 total)
8 squares, 2⅞" × 2⅞"; cut the squares in half diagonally to yield 16 small triangles (192 total)

From the green floral, cut:
16 strips, 3½" × 42"; crosscut into:
    12 strips, 3½" × 23"
    24 strips, 3½" × 10¼"
4 strips, 1½" × 42"; crosscut into 104 squares, 1½" × 1½"

From the red solid, cut:
3 strips, 2" × 42"; crosscut into 52 squares, 2" × 2"

From the tan print, cut:
4 squares, 16" × 16"; cut the squares into quarters diagonally to yield 16 setting triangles

From the red floral, cut:
8 strips, 4½" × 42"
9 strips, 2½" × 42"

Making the Blocks

Press the seam allowances as indicated by the arrows.

1. Using a rotary cutter, mat, and the 45° line on an acrylic ruler, trim one end of a red 2½" × 20" strip at a 45° angle. Rotate the strip so the cut edge is on your left. Cutting parallel to the trimmed edge, cut four diamonds, 2½" wide.

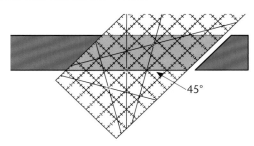

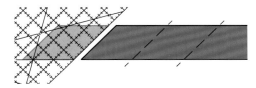

Cut 4 diamonds from strip.

2. Repeat step 1 to cut 24 sets of four matching red diamonds and 24 sets of four matching green diamonds.

3. For one Star block, gather a set of four matching red and four matching green diamonds, as well as eight large triangles and eight small triangles from a single light print.

4. Sew a small light triangle to the top-left edge of a red diamond as shown. Add a large light triangle to the top-right edge to make a star-point unit. Repeat to make four matching star-point units.

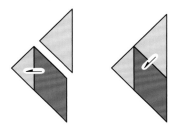

Make 4 star-point units.

5. Paying close attention to orientation and using a green diamond, add triangles to the diamond to make a mirror-image star-point unit. Make four mirror-image star-point units.

Make 4 mirror-image star-point units.

6. Sew together a star-point unit and a mirror-image star-point unit to make a quarter block. The block should measure 5⅜" square, including seam allowances. Repeat to make four matching quarter blocks.

Make 4 quarter blocks, 5⅜" x 5⅜".

7. Lay out the quarter blocks in two rows of two blocks. Sew the blocks into rows, and then join the rows to complete a Star block. The block should measure 10¼" square, including seam allowances. Make 24 Star blocks.

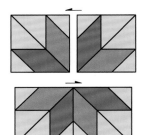
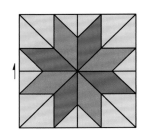

Make 24 Star blocks, 10¼" x 10¼".

Susan says...

I based the setting for this quilt on an antique. Did you notice that the green sashing doesn't crisscross at the four corners? Do you think the maker of the antique one ran out of fabric? At any rate, I didn't use antique methods. There are no, nada, zero Y seams in this quilt. I love making LeMoyne Stars the easy way!

Making the Sashing Units

1 Use a pencil to mark a diagonal line on the wrong side of each green 1½" square. Align a marked square right sides together on one corner of a red square as shown. Sew on the drawn line. Trim the seam allowances to ¼". Add a second marked square to the opposite corner of the red square as shown. Make 52 sashing units.

Make 52,
2" x 2".

2 Lay out four units from step 1 in two rows as shown. Sew together the units in each row. Join the rows to make a sashing square. Make 13, each 3½" square, including seam allowances.

Make 13 sashing squares,
3½" x 3½".

Assembling the Quilt Top

1 Referring to the assembly diagram on page 79, lay out the blocks, sashing squares, tan setting triangles, green floral 3½" × 23" sashing strips, and green floral 3½" × 10¾" sashing strips in diagonal rows.

2 In the upper-left and lower-right corners, sew the setting triangles to the adjacent block as shown. Then sew together the pieces in the diagonal rows. Join the rows.

3 Carefully trim the quilt top ¼" beyond the points of each block. The quilt top should measure 68½" square.

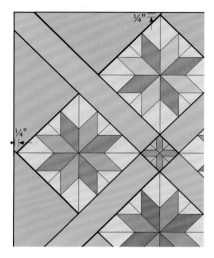

Adding the Border

1 Join the red 4½" × 42" strips end to end and press the seam allowances open. Trim the pieced length into two 76½"-long border strips and two 68½"-long border strips.

2 Sew the shorter border strips to the sides of the quilt top, and then add the longer strips to the top and bottom edges. The completed quilt top should measure 76½" square.

Finishing the Quilt

Find free, detailed finishing instructions online at ShopMartingale.com/HowtoQuilt.

1 Prepare the quilt backing so it is about 8" larger in both directions than the quilt top.

2 Layer the backing, batting, and quilt top. Baste the layers together.

3 Hand or machine quilt as desired; the quilt shown is machine quilted with an allover paisley-and-circle design.

4 Using the red floral 2½"-wide strips, make the binding and attach it to the quilt.

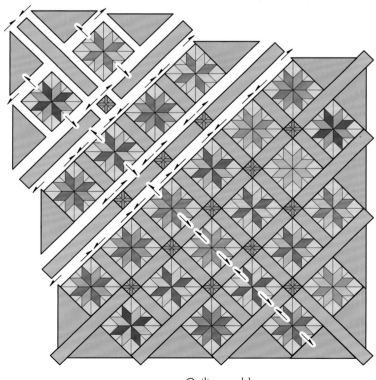

Quilt assembly

About the Author

Knowing only that she wanted to feature embroidery and Nine Patch blocks, Susan Ache taught herself to make her first quilt. Quiltmaking opened up a new world to this mom of five now-grown children. She turned many hours reading about quiltmaking into a lifelong passion for creating beautiful quilts.

Susan finds color inspiration in her native Florida surroundings. She's always searching for new and fun ways to show off as many colors as she can in a quilt. Most of her quilts are a creative impulse inspired by a trip to the garden center, a photograph in a magazine, or a few paint color swatches. She never sees just the quilt—she sees the room where the quilt belongs.

Working in a quilt store for years helped cultivate Susan's love of color and fabric. Visit Susan on Pinterest and Instagram as @yardgrl60.

3.4 *Risposte possibili:* a. Sembra che una macchina stia uscendo dal garage, invece è un disegno | b. Sembra che il rubinetto sia sospeso in aria, invece è una fontana | c. Sembra che l'uomo sia dentro a una piscina, invece è sotto a un vetro | d. Sembra che l'uomo sia in bicicletta, invece è un disegno.

3.5 a. *Che casino!*, Non me ne frega niente, Mi fa schifo, Non mi rompere le scatole. | b. Che confusione!, Non mi interessa, Non mi piace, Non mi disturbare.

4.1 1. toc toc | 2. sssh | 3. patapum | 4. clic | 5. boom | 6. tac.

4.2 a. è nel pallone | b. sbracciandosi | c. azzardo | d. geme | e. abisso esistenziale | f. in doppia fila davanti a noi | *Come si risolverebbe la questione a Roma?* c

4.3 a. ◉◉◉○○; b. ◉◉◉◉◉; c. ◉○○○○

4.4 a/2 | b/3 | c/1

5.1 1. scopa | 2. tatuaggi | 3. barba | 4. bicchiere | 5. piatti | 6. bottiglia

5.2 1/c | 2/b | 3/f | 4/d | 5/e | 6/a

UNITÀ 14 – OSPITALITÀ DEL SUD

1.1 2

1.2 c

3.1 affettuoso, abbondante, allegramente, pigiama, materassini, disagio, ospitalità, invitarli, tranquillamente

3.2 1. c | 2. b

3.3 1. a | 2. c | 3. b

4.1 **Offrire:** *a*, d, e | **Rifiutare:** b, c, f

4.2 1/b | 2/e | 3/a | 4/f | 5/c

4.3 1. affittare | 2. feriale | 3. ospite | 4. tirare

4.4 1/c | 2/b | 3/d | 4/a

5.2 Gli ospiti sono sempre graditi: o quando vengono o quando se ne vanno.

15. UNA LINGUA MISTERIOSA

1.1 1. a | 2. b | 3. a | 4. c | 5. b | 6. a | 7. a | 8. c

3.1 V: 1, 3, 6, 7, 8, 10 | F: 2, 4, 5, 9

3.2 *Risposta libera*

3.3 1/a | 2/c | 3/e | 4/h | 5/d | *6/g* | 7/i | 8/f | 9/b

4.1 a. insalata di polpo | b. baccalà mantecato | c. schie con la polenta | d. baccalà vicentino | e. sarde in saor | f. tramezzini

4.2 a. 1 | b. 4 | c. 3 | d. 6 | e. 5 | f. 7 | g. 2

4.3 a. 5.000, 30.000, *1000*, 500 | b. 1, 2.000, 6.000 | c. *423*, 80, 3.2, 2008 | d. *116*, 4, 50.000

5.1 1. *spargimento di sangue* | 2. barcollava | 3. scompostamente | 4. Fiat Tipo | 5. felici come pasque | 6. innocuo | 7. lugubri | 8. percuotere

5.2 al nostro banco, in spiaggia, una bolla di sapone, scompartimento, disponibili, bicchiere, fastidio, ridotto, ampio, appiccicoso, freddo, sguardi.

[LIVELLO B2]

16. BUROCRAZIA

3.1 1/c | 2/a | 3/d | 4/e | 5/b

3.2 1/e | 2/c | 3/b | 4/a | 5/d | 6/f

3.4 *Si può aggiungere **ma** nelle frasi* 1, 3, 4, 6, 7

4.1 1. C | 2. E | 3. E | 4. P | 5. C | 6. E | 7. C

4.2 opere, sinonimo, assurdo, sensazione, consueti.

4.3 *L'oggetto descritto in corsivo è:* a 1/confusi | 2/treno veloce | 3/arrogante | 4/società segreta | 5/burocrati | 6/molto divertente | 7/stupida | 8/assurdità | 9/pietre

4.4 1/d | 2/a | 3/c | 4/b

5.1 1. a | 2. a | 3. b | 4. a | 5. b | 6. a | 7. b | 8. a | 9. b | 10. b | 11. b | 12. a

5.2 1/c | 2/a | 3/d | 4/b | 5/f | 6/e

17. AMORE DI MAMMA

1.1 a/4 | b/6 | c/1 | d/5 | e/2 | f/3

3.1 *1/c* | 2/b | 3/a | 4/d | 5/e

3.2 1

3.3 *Risposte possibili:* a. Siete venuti a trovare il cugino di Piero | b. "Oggi è rimasto a casa *perché non si sente bene / ha mal di pancia"* | c. "Hai finito il latte? Vuoi qualcos'altro?" | d. È meglio se ti copri se non stai bene. Vuoi che vada a prenderti la sciarpa?"

3.4 ino, etto | 1/berrettino | 2/biscottino | 3/braccialettino | 4/ciabattina | 5/ contrattino; 6/fettina | 7/mandarinetto | 8/mulinetto | 9/giardinetto | 10/rubinettino | 11/spinetta | 12/bambinetto

3.5 1/*Peppino* | 2/Leonardino | 3/Robertino | 4/Carletto | 5/Pierino | 6/Giacomino | 7/Riccardino | 8/Tommasino | 9/Giulietta | 10/Giorgina | 11/Paoletta | 12/Chiaretta | 13/Annina | 14/Franceschina | 15/Lauretta | 16/Michelina *(NOTA: Ci possono essere delle variazioni a seconda della regione italiana)*

3.6 parlata, più

4.1 *La risposta fuori tema è quella di **Ciambella**.*

4.2 1/mai vista | 2/ingannevole | 3/non ti lasciano spazio | 4/combattuti | 5/asilo per i bambini da 0 a 3 anni | 6/mal di schiena | 7/terribile, di morte | 8/riportare con forza | 9/colpo. | a. ghiaia | b. merendine | c. ginocchia sbucciate | d. astuccio | e. catena sporca della bici | f. odore degli alberi

5.1 3. *Lupingu Iwa Cibola* | 4. *Migrant mother* | 5. La *Pietà* è stata restaurata diverse volte nella sua lunga storia, in particolare nel 1972 dopo un atto vandalico.

18. MCLAMPREDOTTO

1.1 a, c

1.2 a, c, e, f

3.1 2

3.2 a. genuino | b. gustoso | c. economico

4.1 povero, di strada, tradizionale, locale

4.2 1, 3, 4

4.3 *essere un salame* = essere un credulone | *essere una mozzarella* = essere pallido | *essere come il prezzemolo* = essere un impiccione

4.4 1/b | 2/c | 3/a

4.5 Il toro e il fornaio/d | Il sogno premonitore/c | Il miracolo dell'albero fiorito/b | La caduta della palla/a

5.1 a/mango | b/zenzero | c/acqua | d/vino | 5/tè verde

5.2 a/Argentina | b/Iran | c/Giamaica | d/Giappone | e/Costa d'Avorio | f/Croazia

19. TESORI NASCOSTI

1.1 a

3.1 1/b | 2/f | 3/d | 4/c | 5/a | 6/e

3.2 Giusy

3.3 c | *Risposte possibili:* 2. Vietato coprirsi il capo | 3. Vietato entrare con animali domestici. | 4. Obbligatorio silenziare la suoneria del telefono. | 5. Vietato scattare foto con il flash. | 6. Vietato entrare con un abbigliamento non decoroso.

4.2 1/b | 2/e | 3/d | 4/c | 5/a

4.3 tachicardia, allucinazioni, bellezza, Firenze, straniera, straordinarie, visita

4.4 1/b | 2/d | 3/a | 4/c

5.1 1/g | 2/d | 3/f | 4/i | 5/c | 6/a | 7/b | 8/e | 9/h

5.2 *Siete* la nave più bella del mondo!

20. IL DERBY

1.1 a. *Genova* | b. Milano | c. Roma | d. Torino | e. Verona | f. Toscana

3.1 V: 1, 2, 7 | F: 3, 4, 5, 6

3.2 c

3.3 b

4.1 a/1 | b/E | c/2 | d/1 | e/1 | f/2

4.2 1/a | 2/d | 3/b | 4/c | 5/f | 6/e

4.3 1. *L'oggetto che sta cercando Val è un fischietto, si trova nel riquadro B1* | 2. *Nel disegno ci sono vari oggetti che si usano nel* tennis, ciclismo, basket, pattinaggio su ghiaccio, boxe

4.4 1/c | 2/d | 3/a | 4/b | 5/e

5.1 a/3 | b/5 | c/1 | d/4 | e/6 | f/2

5.2 *Risposta libera*